MW00446473

"What is the use of a book," thought Alice,

"without pictures or conversations."

Lewis Carroll
<u>Alice's Adventures in Wonderland</u>

Happy Travels!
Daniel R. Frew

52 Weekends in the Tennessee Valley

Charles T. Frew and Daniel R. Frew

Copyright © 2006, Frew and Associates, Incorporated

All rights reserved. No part of this book shall be reproduced or transmitted in any form or by any means, electronic, mechanical, magnetic, photographic including photocopying, recording or by any information storage and retrieval system, without prior written permission of the authors. No patent liability is assumed with respect to the use of the information contained herein. Although every precaution has been taken in the preparation of this book, the authors assume no responsibility for errors or omissions. Neither is any liability assumed for damages resulting from the information contained herein.

ISBN 0-9777415-0-8

Printed by McQuiddy Printing Company, Nashville, Tennessee.

With the exception of the helmetcam skydiving photo on page 106, all of the photography in this publication was taken by either Charles or Daniel Frew.

www.tennesseevalleybook.com

Introduction

In *Requiem for a Nun*, Mississippi novelist William Faulkner wrote, "The past isn't dead. It's not even past." Faulkner may well have been thinking about the Deep South and its many historical characteristics when he made that observation. *52 Weekends in the Tennessee Valley* provides a light-hearted commentary on the many historical, geographical, and remarkable qualities that make this region of the country truly spectacular. As you read this book, you will find the Tennessee Valley's traditions and heritage intertwine with the modern world to yield a revolving mosaic of rich, colorful images. Fascinating people, unique pastimes, delectable foods – we are fortunate to be living in such a colorful neck of the woods! From coonskin caps and cornbread to space programs and sorghum festivals, marvelous opportunities abound in the Valley area. The definition of the Tennessee Valley's boundaries depends on who you ask, and the area's annual events often shuffle dates from year to year. Therefore, this book does not showcase a particular event every single weekend of the year. Instead, we've presented a multitude of exciting local attractions and events for you to visit as you see fit.

Whether you are a music fan, Civil War buff, biker, hiker, or art lover, the Valley offers plenty to keep you smiling. We also encourage you to read local newspapers, contact chambers of commerce, and check regional and community Internet Web sites to identify current activities, attractions, and points of interest. Remember – opportunities are seldom labeled, so after you've read something that catches your eye, seize the day and *experience* the Tennessee Valley!

Contents

CHAPTER I:
Exploring the Tennessee Valley
Reasons to Go and Boundaries to Define

Over the Hills and Far Away

The Tennessee Valley – what an incredible place to live. So many lively activities, so many interesting places to visit. And you don't have to be Marco Polo to check them out! In fact, all you really need is a little energy and a free weekend. This area provides plenty of reasons to travel, and rest assured that all of your books, TV programs, and telephone messages will be there upon your return.

Before booking a flight for an out-of-town vacation, consider visiting some of the attractions found right up the road. You might be surprised at what awaits. For example, by the time you finish reading this publication, you will know where in the Tennessee Valley to find African Elephants, Greek statues, Italian architecture, and Japanese gardens – all with none of the jetlag! People from all around the world travel to this region for barbeque competitions, music festivals, and informative museums. Alabama and Tennessee each pull in hundreds of millions of dollars every year in tourism revenue. People are coming here, so pack a lunch and go see what the fuss is all about.

Staying Young at Heart

A few years ago, at the age of 77, former Senator John Glenn launched into space aboard the shuttle *Discovery*. Can an individual's twilight years get much more exciting? Unfortunately, it seems as most people grow older, their level of enthusiasm and sense of adventure tend to fade. In turn, children, aside from taking baths and doing homework, look forward to just about everything. In the summertime, they play for hours in the sprinklers. In the fall they play in enormous piles of raked leaves. In the winter, kids bundle up and get out of the house to throw the football or make snow angels, and in the springtime it's a search for birds' nests or lightning bugs. But time passes, and children grow up. While they were at one time happy to explain to anyone that they were "four and a half," eventually they *turn* 21, *become* 30, *push* 40, *reach* 50 and *make it* to 60. After that, they *hit* 70, and then, strangely, begin bragging about how young they are! Age is indeed a unique institution. Old age has been described by some as an infinite period of time approximately 15 years older than the person defining it. Regardless of when you consider old age to commence, suffice it to say that few of us truly live life to the fullest. As we grow older, it is natural for us to spend more time thinking about the past. What we *do not* have to do, however, is stop living for the present! So put away the Metamucil and prune juice and get out your highlighter and map. Simply put, there is just no time like the present.

> *"You don't stop laughing because you grow old. You grow old because you stop laughing."*
>
> **Michael Pritchard**
> **Motivational Speaker**

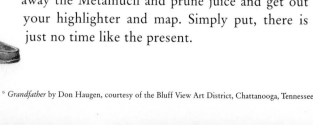

* *Grandfather* by Don Haugen, courtesy of the Bluff View Art District, Chattanooga, Tennessee

Rescuing Your Loved Ones From the Family's Safe House

Norman Rockwell once painted a two-frame picture, entitled *Going and Coming*, which subsequently appeared on the cover of *The Saturday Evening Post*. The first picture depicts a family, including the dog and grandmother, heading out in their car to who knows where. Except for the grandmother, who looks totally impassive, excitement and anticipation can be seen on all their faces. The next frame shows the same family on the return leg of their trip. This time the family, including the dog, looks exhausted, sunburned, and anxious to get home. The only person who looks exactly the same is the grandmother, who obviously endured the outing with minimum stress.

When planning a weekend outing for the family, all members must first defeat both the Inertia and Comfort Zone monsters. The Inertia monster tempts family members to remain on the sofa for hours on end, engrossed with whatever is on the tube. The Internet, PlayStation®, and Blockbuster® membership – these things all fuel our tendency to miss out on the outside world. The Comfort Zone monster has created invisible walls around entire neighborhoods, preventing us from venturing out and exploring new horizons. Fortunately for us, these two should be no match for the abundance of wonderful life experiences awaiting knowledgeable Tennessee Valley inhabitants! As inventive as *Seinfeld* rerun storylines are, can they compare with the originality of the RC Cola and MoonPie Festival in Bell Buckle, Tennessee? Given a choice between watching a movie about *Apollo 13*, or jetting over to Huntsville where you can see an actual Apollo capsule, why not go see the real thing?

When you do mobilize the troops and venture out for that weekend trip, chances are that some of your loved ones might react like the younger family members in Rockwell's painting. Others, like the grandmother, will remain cool, collected, and relaxed throughout it all. It is important to accept such mini-vacations without emotionally self-destructing over the unknown challenges that might occur. Simply try to keep your travel experiences – both good and bad – in perspective, and always embrace the adventure.

Are We There Yet?

Author and television journalist Charles Kuralt once noted in his book *On the Road* that, "Thanks to the interstate highway system, it is now possible to travel from coast to coast without seeing anything." Many people believe that interstate highways take the adventure out of traveling. We suggest when starting out on a weekend excursion, take a leisurely, scenic route to your destination. The quickest, most direct route should be reserved only for the return trip when everyone is tired and eager to return to friends and familiar surroundings. Once you've identified the initial route, estimate how much time it will take to reach your destination via the back roads, then add a few hours to the timetable. This allows for some free exploration time, in case you happen upon any unexpected curiosities.

If the driving route to the destination involves primarily interstate travel, the scenery might be limited to corny bumper stickers and ugly billboards decorating the roadway. And beware of runaway herds of tractor trailers and big-rigs on the interstate.

Back roads also present their own challenges. Anyone who has lived in the region for any length of time has found themselves on a two-lane highway behind a slow-moving pickup or mobile-home caravan. In fact, throughout the Deep South, you can encounter a variety of travel dilemmas. When taking a trip during harvest season, you will find the

> *"In America, there are two classes of travel – first class and with children."*
> **Robert Benchley**
> **Author and Humorist**

> *"Never go on trips with anyone you do not love."*
> **Ernest Hemingway**

roads filled with an armada of farm vehicles, combines, cotton harvesters, and tractor-towed wagons. Sprinkled throughout these agrarian parades are backhoe vehicles, which creep along at breakneck speeds of up to 20 miles per hour. At times it seems these vehicles are mechanically incapable of pulling off to the side of the road to allow the angry string of motorists behind them to pass. Another regional traveling challenge involves chickens. Someday you might very well find yourself directly behind a truck transporting numerous cages of our feathered friends to the local processing plant. This is an experience few people outside the South can truly appreciate. These poor chickens, with their heads protruding from the cages, are truly a pathetic sight to behold. The aromatic odors, accompanied by the continuous shower of feathers, can be a real wake-up call to drowsy or inattentive drivers. Additionally, Tennessee Valley travelers face the challenge of driving on football or racing weekends. When such events take place, you should be on constant lookout for crazed fanatics and their erratic driving, giant flapping flags, and excited, loyal passengers. Limbs protrude from car windows, and truck beds overflow with enthusiastic supporters!

"Two roads diverged in a wood and I – I took the one less traveled by, and that has made all the difference."

Robert Frost
"The Road Not Taken"

National insurance institutes routinely point to statistics showing that Boston, Massachusetts, may be the most dangerous place to drive in the United States. The driving reputations of these Northeastern drivers are based on many reasons. One reason is a common inability to slow their living and driving paces down to what Southerners consider "normal" speeds. In that part of the country, drivers are often confronted with overly congested freeways and a proliferation of "rotaries," also known as "round-abouts." Rotaries are simply large, circular intersections that have multiple entry and exit points. Fortunately, Tennessee Valley drivers habitually drive on uncongested rural roads and are completely knowledgeable when it comes to the navigation of rotaries. Any Southerner born in the Valley probably spent most weekend evenings of his or her teenage years driving around the local county courthouse squares for hours, in search of social opportunities. The only difference between these Southern locations and those used by Northerners is that one is a square, and the other is a circle. Also, Southerners don't have high numbers of recordable accidents like our Northern counterparts do. The reason for this is simple – few Southerners will jump to contact the local sheriff's department to report an accident involving two or more old pickup trucks.

"Make voyages! Attempt them! There's nothing else ..."

Tennessee Williams

Regional Rules of the Road

The following vehicles have the right-of-way at a four-way stop:

1. A vehicle with a weapon pointed out the window

2. A vehicle that fishtails into the intersection

3. A vehicle displaying at least two confederate flags, and has extremely large tires – but is missing a windshield

4. A vehicle that has either an animal or a spouse tied across the hood

All of the above should be given the widest berth possible and be allowed to proceed without argument, horn-blowing, or finger waving!

On your trip through the Valley, stopping at interstate rest areas should be strictly controlled and monitored. Children should not be allowed to spend all of their money at the first vending machine they see, nor should they be allowed to play hide-and-seek in alternating bathrooms. After you've collected every available local travel brochure, count noses to make sure that all family members are accounted for and that no one is trying to leave with a stray pet he or she has recently befriended. Prior to departing the rest area, verify that little ones who had previously been screaming about urgently needing to use the facilities actually did.

If you are a non-resident traveling through the Valley, you may be forced to make an adjustment or two – from our pace of life and dialect to our love of college football, for some people this region takes a little getting used to. Things can be different here, but those differences are the very things we cherish! If newcomers can adjust just a little, then they, like all Valley residents, will have plenty to enjoy. The key is to get out and explore.

In Search of the Tennessee Valley

Does anyone really know where the Tennessee Valley is? Just as you cannot specifically define the precise parameters of Bayou Country or the Great Plains, the same dilemma applies to identifying the location of the Tennessee Valley. Within Tennessee, there are two geographical watersheds: the Cumberland River Watershed, which is in Kentucky and Tennessee, and the Tennessee River Watershed, which extends down from Tennessee into northern Alabama. Geographic charts clearly show the Cumberland watershed to extend south below Nashville, and into the area popularly known as "middle Tennessee." Conversely, other publications note that middle Tennessee, including Nashville, clearly lies between the eastern and western "arms" of the rambling Tennessee River. Notwithstanding the Cumberland River and watershed forms its own valley, many periodicals (perhaps incorrectly) refer to the entire area between the "arms" as being in the Tennessee Valley. Using this interpretation, the Tennessee Valley covers parts of at least two states and encompasses not only a valley, but also canyons, mountains, and plateaus. Although its namesake, the Tennessee Valley Authority (TVA), has jurisdiction to sell power to 8.5 million customers in a region that reaches parts of seven states, such a large area realistically could not be described as being *in* the Tennessee Valley. Although no one really knows the actual boundaries of the "Valley," everyone in this area thinks they live in it. It should be accepted, however, that the Valley does not include either Iowa or Hawaii.

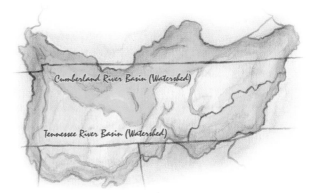

Tennessee Valley Watersheds

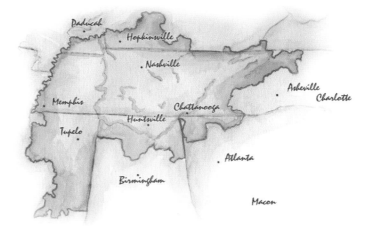

Tennessee Valley Authority (TVA) Jurisdiction

Boundaries Defined

The region of the Tennessee Valley to be discussed in this book starts at a nonexistent point in Nashville (which falls clearly within the Cumberland watershed) and extends both east and west along U.S. Federal Route 40, until it reaches the Tennessee River. The river makes a large U-shape around Tennessee and northern Alabama. Our discussion of the Valley encompasses the area that goes south along both sections of this river. On the eastern side, the river acts as the boundary proceeding south through Chattanooga, Tennessee, touching the tip of Georgia at Chickamauga, and then continuing on into Alabama. Far to the west of Nashville, the boundary runs south along the river, diverts at Pickwick Lake, dropping straight south until the boundary reaches U.S. Highway 78 near Hamilton, Alabama. At that point it proceeds east, and with a few exceptions, follows Federal highways 278 and 74 until it reaches the Alabama/Georgia state line. Our boundary then proceeds due north until it again meets up with the Tennessee River south of Chattanooga. By considering the Valley to extend generally from Nashville to somewhere just past Cullman, Alabama, we cover many areas that might otherwise have been excluded. Although many could challenge this area of concentration, we have chosen to feature the locations and events in this general region for this publication.

Taking the Gamble to Discover What is Over the Mountain

Have you ever heard the saying, "You have to kiss a lot of frogs before you find your prince (or princess)?" Well, it's the same with venturing out to visit locations and festivals – many times you have no idea what awaits you. Sometimes the weekend destination turns out to be either completely overrated or a total disappointment. Perhaps it will be at a seafood festival that you discover your allergic reaction to crawfish. Or maybe it will be right after paying the entry fee at the art museum that your child throws a world-class tantrum. That's life! Fortunately, just as often as disaster strikes, destinations can prove so wonderful and interesting that you choose to return again and again. Columbus was looking for a faster trade route to India when he stumbled across the Bahamas. Who knows what surprises – big and small – await you! Your biggest thrill of the week might involve finding a 60-year-old magazine at one of the many antique shops peppering the back roads of Tennessee and Alabama. Maybe the music at a festival is just plain awful, but while waiting in line to buy some roasted corn you strike up a conversation with a stranger and have a few laughs. In any event, you will always form some opinion about your weekend adventure that you can later discuss with a neighbor or coworker. The most important thing is that you ventured out and went exploring! That, in itself, speaks loudly for you.

"A nation which does not remember what it was yesterday does not know where it is today."

Robert E. Lee

Contrasts and Contradictions

The Tennessee Valley, from a global perspective, is the relative new kid on the block. Its history does not run as deep, as say, that of Rome or Cairo. The history we claim is our own, and as brief as it may be we can still appreciate its better points, wince at its sadder points, and learn from everything in between. Conversely, surrounding every museum, Civil War battlefield, and steam-powered automobile, wonderful examples of modern technology and forward thinking abound. While the cotton fields of Huntsville are largely responsible for putting it on the map, they now play second fiddle to a space, engineering and defense industry that sets standards on a global scale. Just to the south of Nashville's breathtaking skyline lie a dozen landmark antebellum homes. As your travels in the Valley lead you from the pioneer homes to the ultra-modern art galleries, here's hoping you emerge with some fantastic memories and a richer knowledge of what was, what is, and what is yet to come!

CHAPTER II:
The Valley of Long Ago
Indians, Pioneers, and Settlers

Looking Back

From Mound Builders to carpetbaggers, the Tennessee Valley has seen a multitude of changes with the passage of time. When one studies the Valley's evolution, that person realizes that there are no easily defined periods of demarcation. American Indian tribes were transitional, as were the pioneers in their persistent march to the frontier lands. Early settlers strived to obtain land and develop communities for their families. In the time leading up to the antebellum period (before the Civil War), treaties, conflicts, and painful resolutions were all part of the changing tapestry that cloaked the Valley for centuries. Only by understanding some of the area's past events and its people can we better appreciate what the Tennessee Valley is today.

Our Region's Earliest Inhabitants

No one knows how long man has inhabited the Tennessee Valley. Archaeologists divide the prehistoric cultures of the region into four distinct stages: the Paleo (10000 B.C. to 7000 B.C.), Archaic (7000 B.C. to 1000 B.C.), Woodland (1000 B.C. to A.D. 800), and Mississippian (A.D. 800 to A.D. 1500.) It is estimated that Indians first occupied modern-day Tennessee and Alabama during the last ice age around 15,000 years ago. The first inhabitants of the Tennessee basin were Paleo-Indians. They were nomadic hunters who used stone-tipped spears and cooked their food in open pits. These Indians eventually settled near the Muscle Shoals, Alabama, area.

The Mound Builders

Beginning with the prehistoric Copena Indians, many tribes in the Valley eventually became "Mound Builders." Earthen walls often encircled these mounds. The mounds were quite large, some with "flat tops" measuring up to an entire acre. Commonly used as the chiefs' home, the mounds were also used for ceremonial, religious, social, and cultural purposes. This practice lasted for many years. In Oakville, Alabama, you can find remains of more than 20 mounds in the surrounding area.

Tribes of the Valley

The story of Indians and early settlers of the Tennessee Valley is a story of the Tennessee River itself. The river ran southwest from what is now Tennessee into Alabama, then northwest through Muscle Shoals back into Tennessee, and then north into Kentucky. In early times, the Tennessee River was totally unpredictable concerning seasonal navigation and commerce. Because it made a huge "U" into northern Alabama, early settlers referred that part of the river as the "Great Hook" or "Great Bend."

Most of the area's Indian tribes located their villages along the river, which provided them with a primary means of transportation between these various locations. All tribes practiced agriculture, were quite mobile, and often subdivided into various groups for many reasons. Tribes often changed their names as their economic and social needs changed. The "Five Civilized Tribes" – Cherokee, Seminole, Choctaw, Creek, and Chickasaw – were located in the southeast United States and throughout the Valley. They were labeled civilized because they became highly advanced in the ways of the white man.

Smaller tribes also resided in the area. Some members of the Cherokee tribe split from their original band and renamed themselves the Chickamauga. The Shawnee, a nomadic tribe, established villages near what is now Nashville. The Yuchi tribe lived in the mountains of eastern Tennessee and eventually relocated on the Tennessee River around Muscle Shoals. Because of the unbroken forest and waterways, the various tribes used the entire Tennessee Valley area as a general hunting ground. The land and the rivers offered an abundance of food of every kind.

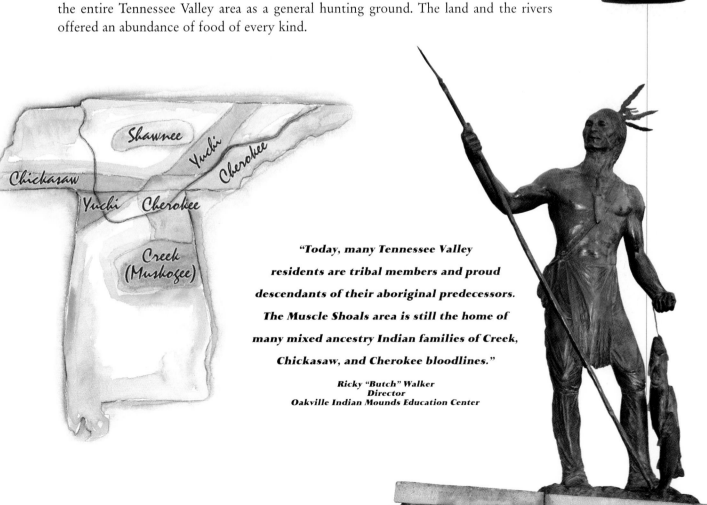

"Today, many Tennessee Valley residents are tribal members and proud descendants of their aboriginal predecessors. The Muscle Shoals area is still the home of many mixed ancestry Indian families of Creek, Chickasaw, and Cherokee bloodlines."

Ricky "Butch" Walker
Director
Oakville Indian Mounds Education Center

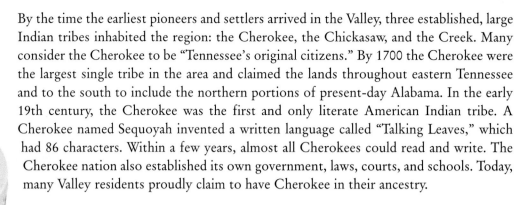

By the time the earliest pioneers and settlers arrived in the Valley, three established, large Indian tribes inhabited the region: the Cherokee, the Chickasaw, and the Creek. Many consider the Cherokee to be "Tennessee's original citizens." By 1700 the Cherokee were the largest single tribe in the area and claimed the lands throughout eastern Tennessee and to the south to include the northern portions of present-day Alabama. In the early 19th century, the Cherokee was the first and only literate American Indian tribe. A Cherokee named Sequoyah invented a written language called "Talking Leaves," which had 86 characters. Within a few years, almost all Cherokees could read and write. The Cherokee nation also established its own government, laws, courts, and schools. Today, many Valley residents proudly claim to have Cherokee in their ancestry.

The Chickasaw lived in parts of northern Alabama and western Tennessee. They enjoyed dance and music. Many wore beads and trinkets. The Chickasaw were also fierce warriors and, centuries earlier, almost annihilated DeSoto's expedition when he tried to enslave 200 Chickasaw warriors to serve as load carriers. Later, they twice drove the Shawnee Indians from the Cumberland Valley and subsequently claimed the greater part of what is now western Tennessee. The tribe also had a strong reputation for organization and cleanliness. The Tennessee basin served as the dividing line between the Chickasaws and the Cherokees at the Muscle Shoals area.

The Creek, a confederacy of Muskogee tribes, were primarily farmers. The tribe lived in central and south Alabama, mostly along the rivers. The Creek followed the Cherokee's lead and compiled written codes of laws in English and became literate in their own language. The tribe was a constant threat to the settlers and conducted many raids on newcomers moving into Alabama. The Tennessee Volunteers, led by Andrew Jackson, fought and eventually defeated the Creek in the bloody Battle of Horseshoe Bend in Alabama in 1814.

HISTORIC INDIANS

Five historic Indian tribes lived in this area. By 1701, the Yuchi were living at the shoals on the Tennessee River. In early 1700s, the Yuchi left, some moving to the Cherokee Nation on the Hiwassee River, TN and others to Chattahoochee River, GA. After a dispute with the Cherokees, some Yuchi moved south to the AL-GA border. Although some Creeks lived in the area by the late 1700s, their lands lay south of the Tennessee Divide. The Treaty of Fort Jackson took Creek lands in southern Lawrence County in 1814. The Shawnees moved to the shoals from the Cumberland and Ohio Rivers. Leftwich (1935) says the Chickasaws and Cherokees forced the Shawnees from the Tennessee Valley in 1721. By 1760, Chickasaws moved into the Tennessee Valley from the west. The Chickasaw Boundary Treaty (10 Jan 1786) gave Chickasaws ownership of the area. In 1769, Cherokees challenged the Chickasaws in the Battle of Chickasaw Oldfields south of Huntsville. By 1770, Cherokees were established in Lawrence County. The Chickasaws and Cherokees lived in peace within the Tennessee Valley until the Turkey Town Treaty of 1816 mandated their removal. Today, descendants of the Creeks, Cherokees, and Chickasaws, among others, live in Lawrence County.

Explorers, Pioneers, and Settlers of the Valley

The first European to encounter the Indians of the interior Southeast was Hernando DeSoto in 1540, whose 500-man Spanish expedition traveled the Tennessee River from Chattanooga to Guntersville, Alabama. This was the first recorded exploration of the Tennessee Valley by white men. In his diaries, DeSoto described large, well-organized villages throughout the Valley controlled by powerful chiefs. After his departure, Indian lifestyles for the next 200 years remained virtually unchanged.

In the 1600s the Tennessee River started to serve as part of an early commerce and trade highway between Mississippi and Charleston, South Carolina. By the 1700s the French were using the Tennessee River as a vital part of their trade routes and established numerous trading posts along the river. Conflicts eventually broke out throughout the Southeast between the French and English who were fighting over the furs gathered by the various Indian tribes. This eventually led to the French and Indian War (1754-1763). In 1763, the Treaty of Paris resulted in the French surrendering all land east of the Mississippi to England. In the meantime, the banks of the entire Tennessee River slowly became settlement areas for early settlers coming from the colonies in Virginia and North Carolina. The first settlers who traveled over the Appalachians into the region were from different ethnic backgrounds, the majority of whom were Irish, Scottish and German.

Many treaties and resulting concessions by the various Indian tribes expanded the land made available to migrating settlers. The area later known as middle Tennessee was the subject of a treaty signed in 1775 when the Cherokee sold a vast wilderness to the colonial governments of North Carolina and Virginia. Numerous treaties were made between the different parties. The U.S. Government, however, broke many of the treaties and continued to take over Cherokee territory. The tribes – resenting past concessions, broken treaties, and continuing encroachment on their hunting grounds – started raiding the major settlements and bloodshed between the two groups lasted for decades. To defend themselves and to provide places of refuge, the early settlers built a series of forts (called "stations") throughout middle Tennessee and along the Tennessee River.

The first organized movement into middle Tennessee was led by General James Robertson and Colonel John Donelson. Robertson led his group overland while Donelson took his group down the Tennessee River. In November of 1779, Robertson led a group of approximately 200 settlers out of Fort Patrick Henry in east Tennessee through the Cumberland Gap into central Kentucky. He then headed south and settled his group in north Tennessee. In the meantime, Donelson brought a 30-boat flotilla of

flatboats down the Tennessee River to present-day Chattanooga, where he was repeatedly attacked by Indians. Donelson eventually reunited with Robertson and together they cleared the land and built a log stockade they called Fort Nashborough. Settlers of Fort Nashborough quickly organized and established an early government in the area. This settlement eventually became modern-day Nashville. Because of his prominent role in all aspects of life in middle Tennessee, James Robertson is rightly honored as the "Father of Tennessee." European groups regularly traveled by the Ohio and Cumberland rivers and slowly settled throughout the middle Tennessee Valley. The Great Trading Path and Nickajack trail became popular routes into the Valley. The flood of colonists wanting land of their own became unstoppable.

In 1796, Tennessee became the 16th state of the Union. Soon afterward, the great migration toward the Mississippi Territory (1798-1819) began. Slowly but surely, settlers moved south, built cabins, and developed communities. Many settlers brought cattle and started farming the entire region, growing corn, wheat, oats and tobacco. Settlers moved south from Fort Loudon (near Knoxville, Tennessee) along the Tennessee River and were attracted to the fertile valleys surrounding what became Lookout Mountain. Chattanooga owes its beginning to its location on the Tennessee River. It was first inhabited by the Chickamauga band of the Cherokee Indians. Soon thereafter, Chattanooga began to grow. Originally called Ross's Landing, the city started out as an Indian trading post, but with the help of new railroad lines soon began evolving into a thriving community. Along with Fort Nashborough, it became a major populated community within the Valley.

Much farther south, settlers slowly moved into modern-day Alabama, both to the north and south of the "Big Bend." If river conditions allowed it, they would travel by boats down the Tennessee River from Chattanooga. Settlers established overland trails and migrated north from Mobile, Alabama, and Georgia. Because of the Valley's rich soil, cotton soon became the crop of choice throughout the area.

In north Alabama, one of the first settlements along the Tennessee River was Fort Deposit, located approximately eight miles north of the present location of Guntersville. Downriver, Ditto Landing – named for John Ditto, who is believed to have been the first

white settler in Madison County (1802) – became a landing for flatboats and keelboats. Because of the defeat of the Creek confederacy and Britain's growing demand for cotton, new settlers poured into the Alabama region, especially from Georgia and Tennessee. In 1820, Decatur, Alabama, lying on the south bank of the Tennessee River, slowly became a strategic point for commercial navigation. Muscle Shoals, Alabama, better known as the "Shoals" area, soon began developing its own populated areas. Nearby Tuscumbia, Alabama, was first inhabited by white settlers in 1815 at the site of an old Cherokee village destroyed by General James Robertson in 1787. All along the river, communities and villages were emerging to meet the influx of new settlers. Settlements throughout the area thrived and Alabama became the 22nd state in 1819. During this migration, the European settlers slowly displaced the original inhabitants of the Tennessee Valley.

"The utmost good faith shall always be observed towards the Indians; their lands and property shall never be taken from them without their consent; and, in their property, rights, and liberty, they shall never be invaded or disturbed, unless in just and lawful wars authorized by Congress."

United States Congress
1789

CREEK INDIAN REMOVAL

Black Warriors' Path played a critical role as a route for Creek Removal. On December 19, 1835, some 511 Creek emigrants passed along the path through present-day Oakville Indian Mounds Park. In September 1836, a group of Creeks left Tallassee in a wagon train of 45 wagons, 500 ponies, and 2,000 Indians. This contingent followed along Black Warriors' Path and passed through the present-day Oakville Indian Mounds Park on September 23, 1836. It's ironic that the route used by General John Coffee's army and Davy Crockett, to defeat the Creeks, was one of the same routes used in Creek Removal. Alabama remains the home of many Creek Indians today.

ERECTED BY
THE ALABAMA INDIAN AFFAIRS COMMISSION
1998

CHEROKEE INDIAN REMOVAL

In the early 1800's, Cherokees of this area were under the leadership of Doublehead and Tahlonteskee. After Doublehead's assassination in 1807, Tahlonteskee notified President Jefferson that he and his people were ready to move west. In 1808, Tahlonteskee and 1,130 followers moved to present-day Dardanelle, Arkansas. That band became known as Cherokees West and later the Old Settlers. The Blue Water-Town Creek Village was the final Alabama home of both Cherokee leaders. Doublehead is supposedly buried in Butler Cemetery on Blue Water Creek in Lauderdale County, Alabama. Alabama remains the home of many Cherokees today.

ERECTED BY
THE ALABAMA INDIAN AFFAIRS COMMISSION
1998

"By the early 1840s, the United States government proclaimed that no Indians were left east of the Mississippi River."

Grace Steele Woodward
The Cherokees

In Search of Yesterday

Based on the latest U.S. census surveys, there are approximately 5,200 Indians located in middle Tennessee and 6,500 in north Alabama. Among others, these include members of the Cherokee, Creek, and Choctaw tribes. Historical markers, burial mounds and Indian shrines preserve their heritage throughout the Valley. Museums in the area, such as the Tennessee Museum in Nashville, Old Stone Fort in Manchester, Tennessee, and the Oakville Indian Mounds in Danville, Alabama, all have outstanding exhibits and artifacts. Some of these date back to the prehistoric Woodland period. Additionally, many annual community Indian festivals throughout the Valley display both the history and culture of the various tribes. Pioneer villages and homesteads such as the one located at Noccalula Falls Park in Gadsden, Alabama, depict early settler life. If you are interested in learning about the first inhabitants of the Tennessee Valley, ample opportunities exist to do so.

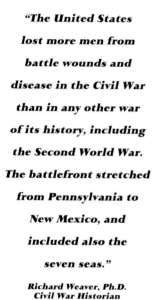

Chapter III: Marching into History
War in the Valley

Solemn Entertainment

In their search for places to visit, weekend Valley adventurers often look no further than their newspapers, travel brochures and paid advertisements for suggested destinations. Many of these attractions and events, however, go out of vogue with the passing of the calendar months. If children are involved, the head of the household often looks for locations and events that provide immediate, visceral entertainment. Older travelers, however, may wish to expand their knowledge about the region and its heritage. If this is the case, spend a weekend learning about how the Civil War physically, emotionally, and economically traumatized the region for decades. In addition to annual reenactments, there are historical areas, homes, trails, markers and state and federal parks throughout the Valley that eloquently detail the events of this tragic story. Notwithstanding the beautifully landscaped parks and visitor centers run by the National Park Service, these are unquestionably some of the Valley's most underrated educational attractions. A little preparation, planning and research prior to visiting these historical landmarks will be worth the time and help visitors better appreciate what they encounter.

Conflict Overview

In December of 1944, America fought the Battle of the Bulge in Belgium. It lasted six weeks and resulted in the largest amount of U.S. deaths in World War II. 19,000 American lives were lost. On February 19, 1945, America invaded Iwo Jima, the first home island to be attacked in the planned invasion of Japan. Nearly 7,000 American soldiers died during the month-long engagement to take the small atoll. Considering casualties and deaths, both were small battles when compared to those of the Civil War. Many Civil War battles lasted less than 48 hours and managed to take more lives through death and disease than the two World War II engagements combined.

It has been said that America's Civil War is among history's most complex conflicts. Between 1861 and 1865, three million Americans took up arms against one another. America became a viciously divided nation. State against state, family against family, and brother against brother. Throughout the nation, the war became an unimaginable bloodbath in which 620,000 lives were lost. Although many people assume the vast majority of conflicts, battles, and skirmishes occurred mostly in the nation's mid-Atlantic states, this is not the case. More battles were fought in Tennessee than any other state except Virginia. There were confrontations throughout the country, extending from Pennsylvania down to the Mississippi coast, and west into Missouri, Kansas, and beyond. The war was not confined to land. Significant naval battles occurred not only on rivers throughout the South, but along the coastlines as well. There was even one battle fought in the English Channel (The Sloop of War, Kearsarge, versus the cruiser C.S.S. Alabama, June 19, 1864).

"The United States lost more men from battle wounds and disease in the Civil War than in any other war of its history, including the Second World War. The battlefront stretched from Pennsylvania to New Mexico, and included also the seven seas."

Richard Weaver, Ph.D.
Civil War Historian

The conflicts in the mid-Atlantic states were generally considered to be in the eastern theater. The western theater was the region between the Appalachian mountains and the Mississippi River. Union forces often named their armies after rivers, and Confederate forces named their armies after geographic regions. This explains why you may occasionally encounter war monuments dedicated to opposing forces such as "Army of Tennessee" and also "Army of the Tennessee." Only by understanding the military situation of the two armies within the Tennessee Valley can you grasp why commanding generals were willing to risk wholesale sacrifices of their troops in an effort to secure this critical region.

"All we ask is to be left alone."
Jefferson Davis

Prologue

From the beginning of the Civil War, the strategy of the Union armies operating west of the Appalachian Mountains centered on two major objectives: gaining control of the Mississippi River and driving a wedge through the Confederacy along the railroads running in a southeastern direction through Tennessee and Georgia. Thus, because of its location, the entire Tennessee Valley eventually became a critical border between the North and South. To the north of the Valley was Tennessee's 300-mile border along the state of Kentucky, which predominately remained loyal to the Union. The major western rivers – the Mississippi, Tennessee, and Cumberland – all provided routes for a military invasion of the South. These combined geographical features resulted in the Valley becoming the military frontline of the Confederacy and a prime battleground of the western theater.

Known as the "Volunteer State," Tennessee was not only the second most populated state in the South, but was also totally split in its loyalties. Many did not support Tennessee's withdrawal from the Union and this resulted in two-third's of its populace in eastern Tennessee remaining pro-Union. Middle and western Tennessee was strongly pro-Confederacy and supplied more soldiers for the Confederacy than any other state except Virginia. Ironically, at the same time it had more of its citizens fight for the Union than all other Southern states combined.

3A   132

NASHVILLE BLACKS IN THE CIVIL WAR

From October - December 1862, on this hill, black laborers helped the Union Army build Fort Negley. In November, blacks helped defend the unfinished fort against Confederate attack. During the Battle of Nashville (December 1864), nearly 13,000 black soldiers aided in the defeat of the Confederates. By 1865, blacks had assisted the Union Army in building 23 fortifications around Nashville.

TENNESSEE HISTORICAL COMMISSION

To a far lesser extent than its neighbor to the north, Alabama's citizens were also divided in their beliefs concerning secession. Many north Alabama men, particularly from Winston and Cullman counties, were anti-secessionist and volunteered to serve the Union. Similar to Tennessee, conflicts raged throughout north Alabama during the entire war. In the fall of 1864, Confederate General John Bell Hood used Tuscumbia as a base for his 38,000-man force prior to his march north to attempt to drive the Union forces out of Nashville. In that region Nathan Bedford Forrest continuously led his cavalry back and forth over the Tennessee River between Alabama and Tennessee to conduct lightning raids against Union-held positions.

"Whenever I hear anyone arguing for slavery, I feel a strong impulse to see it tried on him personally."
Abraham Lincoln

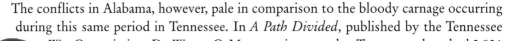

The conflicts in Alabama, however, pale in comparison to the bloody carnage occurring during this same period in Tennessee. In *A Path Divided*, published by the Tennessee War Commission, Dr. Wayne C. Moore points out that Tennessee alone had 2,931 engagements of various sizes. In its fight for control of both railroad lines and rivers, the Union army continuously sent forces in great numbers to what it called the "Keystone of the Southern Arch." Many of the resulting battles were among the bloodiest conflicts in the entire Civil War.

Invasion by Land and River

Major routes of Ulysses S. Grant's Union Army into the Tennessee Valley

"I have never advocated war except as a means of peace."

Ulysses S. Grant

Significant Battles Within the Tennessee Valley

1862
April 6-8
December 31-Jan. 2 (63)

Battle of Shiloh
Battle of Stones River

1863
June 23-July 8
September 18-20
November 23-25

Tullahoma Campaign
Battle of Chickamauga
Battle of Chattanooga

1864
November 30
December 15-16

Battle of Franklin
Battle of Nashville

"As to the comparative value of the two arms of the service, in clearing the western rivers of the Confederates, the Army and the Navy were like blades of shears – united, invincible; separated, almost useless."

**Admiral A.H. Foote
Union Navy**

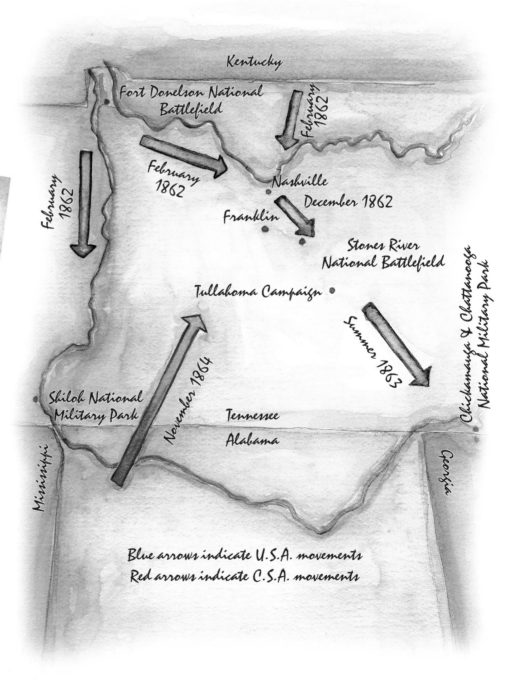

Kentucky

Fort Donelson National Battlefield

February 1862

February 1862

February 1862

Nashville

December 1862

Franklin

Stones River National Battlefield

Tullahoma Campaign

Summer 1863

Chickamauga & Chattanooga National Military Park

Shiloh National Military Park

November 1864

Tennessee

Alabama

Mississippi

Georgia

Blue arrows indicate U.S.A. movements
Red arrows indicate C.S.A. movements

National Civil War Parks in the Valley

Overview

52 Weekends in the Tennessee Valley recommends visits to three Tennessee Civil War battlefields:

- Shiloh National Military Park
- Stones River National Battlefield (Murfreesboro)
- Chickamauga & Chattanooga National Military Park

These battlefields, operated by the National Park Service, have modern visitor centers containing numerous exhibits and video presentations that tell the stories of the battles involved. The historic areas have well-marked driving tours of the battlegrounds. Although the duration of the battles at these three locations lasted a grand total of 12 days, there were approximately 94,370 causalities inflicted on both armies in their struggle to control the Tennessee Valley. When comparing this number to the amount of deaths inflicted throughout the nation during the entire war (620,000), it is clear that the Tennessee Valley was a pivotal junction in the war's outcome.

Nathan Bedford Forrest and the Cavalry That Sank a Naval Force

Although the Civil War produced numerous Union and Confederate generals who graduated from West Point, a Confederate cavalry officer with no prior military experience eventually won enormous respect from both sides for his military tactics and courage. Nathan Bedford Forrest was a slave trader and planter who rose within the Confederacy from a private to lieutenant general. A cavalry soldier who was always in the thick of battle (he had 29 horses shot out from under him), Forrest gained a fearsome reputation for a series of punishing lightning raids against numerous Union strongholds in western and middle Tennessee and northern Alabama. In one battle – Brice's Crossroads, June 10, 1864 – his cavalry of 3,000 men defeated a Union force of more than 8,000 troops. Although there are many stories about Forrest, one tale is unique. On November 4, 1864, at Pilot Knob across from Johnsonville, Tennessee, on the Tennessee River, Forrest directed his cavalry to secretly move artillery into concealed positions on the other side of the river and proceeded to sink an entire fleet of Union gunboats and transports. When the engagement was over, 33 vessels and more than six million dollars of federal property was destroyed. Forrest continued to plague the Union forces until his cavalry corps was forced to surrender on May 9, 1865, near Selma, Alabama. After the war, the Union's General William Tecumseh Sherman said, "He was the most remarkable man our Civil War produced on either side."

*"I saw an open field ...
so covered with dead that
it would have been
possible to walk across
the clearing, in any
direction, stepping on
dead bodies, without a
foot touching the ground."*

**Ulysses S. Grant,
on the Battle of Shiloh**

Battle of Shiloh

April 6-8, 1862

Historians consider the Battle of Shiloh to have been one of the bloodiest conflicts of the entire war. The battle resulted in a casualty rate of 21.6 percent of all forces on the battlefield. During the three days of fighting, Americans sustained more casualties than in the Revolutionary War, the War of 1812, and the Mexican War combined.

General Ulysses S. Grant commanded the Union forces and, following the battles of Fort Henry and Fort Donelson, moved his troops south along the Tennessee River to Pittsburg Landing at Shiloh. The Confederate forces were under the command of General Albert Sidney Johnston. Johnston was hoping to engage Grant's army before it could be reinforced. On April 6, 1862, Johnston launched a powerful attack that drove the Union troops back to an area known as "The Sunken Road." This location was eventually nicknamed "The Hornet's Nest" because of the amount of shells and bullets fired by both sides at point-blank range. Johnston personally led a Confederate attack, but was killed near the end of the first day. Although the Confederates won the first day's battle, that advantage would be fleeting. The Union Army's General Don Carlos Buell later arrived by river, with reinforcements under cover of fire by newly arrived Union gunboats. The Union forces strengthened their line of defense and by the next morning had amassed a combined force of 65,000 men. Unaware of the Union build-up throughout the night, Johnston's replacement, General Pierre Gustave Toutant Beauregard, initiated an unsuccessful attack and was eventually forced to retreat to Corinth. The final number of dead and wounded from this bloody 72-hour engagement was 23,746 soldiers: 13,047 Union and 10,699 Confederate.

Shiloh National Military Park

Established in 1894, Shiloh National Military Park preserves the area of the first major battle in the western theater of the Civil War. The battlefield encompasses approximately 4,000 acres and is located in Hardin County, Tennessee, on the west bank of the Tennessee River. There is an additional park unit located in Corinth, Mississippi, 23 miles southwest of Shiloh. Shiloh National Military Park has been called "the most secluded, best-preserved and most beautiful battlefield in the world."

Battle of Stones River

December 31, 1862 – January 2, 1863

In the fall of 1862, Union armies occupied Nashville and the western half of Tennessee. In October, Confederate forces, under the controversial General Braxton Bragg, went into winter quarters at Murfreesboro, Tennessee. Union Major General William S. Rosecrans's 14th Army Corps (soon to be renamed The Army of the Cumberland) left Nashville on December 26, 1862, with 43,000 men, intending to destroy Bragg's forces and then march directly into Chattanooga. By December 31, 1862, two opposing armies totaling 81,000 men faced each other in battle for control of middle Tennessee.

The battle raged for three days (primarily on December 31 and January 2). A total of 23,515 men were killed, wounded, or captured (USA 13,249; CSA 10,266). The dead and dying filled areas such as the "Slaughter Pen" and "Hell's Half Acre." After the battle, most of the deceased were buried on the field, later to be interred in the Stones River National Cemetery. Only Union dead were buried in this cemetery. Tactically indecisive, The Battle of Stones River provided a much-needed morale boost to the North. It also resulted in Bragg withdrawing his Confederate forces from Murfreesboro. Like Shiloh, this battle was one of the bloodiest encounters of the Civil War.

> *"You gave us a hard-earned victory which, had there been a defeat instead, the nation could hardly have lived over."*
>
> **Abraham Lincoln**

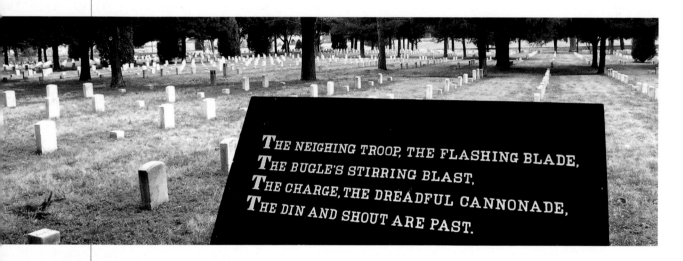

THE NEIGHING TROOP, THE FLASHING BLADE,
THE BUGLE'S STIRRING BLAST,
THE CHARGE, THE DREADFUL CANNONADE,
THE DIN AND SHOUT ARE PAST.

Civil War Reenactments

In addition to visiting Civil War parks and battlefields in the valley, travelers should consider attending one of the many local reenactments of Civil War battles. These reenactments range from large engagements, such as Shiloh and Franklin in Tennessee, to smaller conflicts such as Decatur and Bridgeport in Alabama. Such events provide an entertaining glimpse into the culture-rich past of the Tennessee Valley.

Stones River National Battlefield

A 600-acre site established on March 3, 1927, the Stones River National Battlefield was designated as a national battlefield on April 22, 1960. The area encompasses only a small part of the original battlefield. Within the grounds lie the Stones River National Cemetery, which has more than 6,000 Union graves. The site features a modern visitor center, a bookstore, and a theater, which continuously shows a short video of a reenactment of the battle. Located on the Old Nashville Highway outside Murfreesboro, Tennessee, the battlefield's major points of interest can be seen on a self-guided auto tour that contains numbered markers, short trails, and exhibits.

Battle of Chickamauga

September 18-20, 1863

Six months after the Union force's victory at Stones River, Rosecrans's 70,000-man Army of the Cumberland moved from Murfreesboro, Tennessee, to again engage Confederate General Braxton Bragg's Army of Tennessee. During this period, Bragg's forces had grown to more than 66,000 men. The massive armies finally clashed at Chickamauga, a nondescript area located on a key road south of Chattanooga. Both armies were attempting to permanently occupy Chattanooga, a city then of 2,500 people, and a critical rail center and gateway to the heart of Confederacy. On September 19, 1863, a bitter fight ensued, often with hand-to-hand combat, along a battle line extending more than four miles. Although the Union horse-mounted infantry was now armed with new Spencer repeating rifles that inflicted heavy causalities, Bragg's forces eventually pushed the Federals back. The next day, after a major mistake by the Union forces, troops led by Confederate Lieutenant General James Longstreet smashed through the Union line, routing Rosecrans and one-third of his army. Now in disarray, the Union army retreated back to Chattanooga. Although Bragg's staff, especially Longstreet and Nathan Bedford Forrest, heatedly argued to quickly press their advantage and initiate a full-scale attack against the retreating Union forces before they could reorganize, Bragg refused to heed their advice. That decision eventually proved fatal.

Battle of Chattanooga

November 23-25, 1863

Although Bragg did not order an all-out attack on the retreating forces, he did order his troops to cautiously pursue the Union forces. The Confederates eventually occupied Missionary Ridge, Lookout Mountain, and the Chattanooga Valley on the outskirts of the city. They also placed artillery on the heights overlooking the river, which blocked the roads and rail lines leading into the city. Confederate forces now had a stranglehold on the Union army, which Bragg hoped would result in the surrender or starvation of Rosecrans's forces.

The Union situation was critical. Because the siege had to be broken, President Abraham Lincoln ordered Union reinforcements from throughout the country to come to the aid of the Army of the Cumberland. Chattanooga had to be saved at all costs.

Major General Ulysses S. Grant assumed overall command of all forces west of the Appalachians and replaced Rosecrans with Major General George Thomas (the "Rock of Chickamauga") as head of the Army of the Cumberland. To relieve the forces in the city, Union troops quickly opened a logistical route (nicknamed the "Cracker Line") from Bridgeport, Alabama, and supplies started flowing toward the desperate troops. In the third week of November, the Union started its advance to break out of the Confederate noose. Major battles erupted throughout the area – from Orchard Knob to Lookout Mountain ("Battle Above the Clouds") to Missionary Ridge. On November 25, the Confederate line collapsed and Bragg's troops fled first to the rear and later retreated back into Dalton, Georgia. The Union army now controlled not only the city, but also most of Tennessee. Chattanooga was later used as the logistical base for General William Sherman's march into Atlanta.

Chickamauga – called "River of Death" by the Cherokee – had earned its nickname. The battle's human toll was staggering – more than 34,000 killed, wounded, or missing. Chickamauga was the bloodiest battle in the western theater, and the bloodiest two-day battle of the Civil War.

Chickamauga & Chattanooga National Military Park

Between 1890 and 1899, Congress authorized the establishment of four national military parks. The first and largest of these, and the precursor for most other national military and historical parks, was Chickamauga & Chattanooga National Military Park. Dedicated on August 19, 1890, the park consists of more than 8,000 acres, 660 monuments, and a well-marked seven-mile auto tour of the Chickamauga battlefield. It contains a visitor center with numerous exhibits, a media program, a bookstore, and an outstanding military arms museum. You can find the park's headquarters located just south of the Tennessee/Georgia line off of Battlefield Parkway on U.S. Highway 27.

Post-War Years

Anyone knowledgeable about the Civil War knows there was nothing *civil* about it. More than 620,000 lives were lost and every part of the nation was impacted in some way. The South lay in shambles, its economy and many of its cities destroyed. The hatred and bitterness generated from this four-year tragedy was ingrained in families from both the North and South for years to come. In the Tennessee Valley, reconstruction came slowly. Men returned to their businesses, farms, and cotton fields, vowing to regain the prosperity they once enjoyed. "Carpetbaggers" from the North began flowing into the region, introducing new ideas and manufacturing processes previously unknown to Valley residents. Cotton, farming, commerce, banking, and textiles became economic cornerstones of many towns and villages throughout the region. Political parties became defined, and the Ku Klux Klan came into being. Unions were introduced to the labor forces and religious and social organizations began to shape communities throughout the Valley. The new war of capitalism had begun.

"The South hasn't disappeared. If anything, it's become more Southern in a last-ditch effort to save itself. And the South that survives will last longer than the one that preceded it. It'll be harder and more durable than what came before. Why? It's been through the fire."

Dennis Covington
<u>Salvation on Sand Mountain</u>

CHAPTER IV:
Traits of the Valley
From Antiques to Zydeco

Sights and Geography

When exploring the Tennessee Valley, you may often observe numerous regional symbols that reflect not only the spirit and personality of the area, but that of the Deep South itself. From small tornado shelters that resemble underground forts to old-fashioned country stores found at many Valley crossroads, these cultural icons set the South apart from the rest of the country. Red barns with "See Rock City" painted on their roofs are still around – although gradually disappearing. Additionally, you can still find clapboard and "shotgun" houses, often with appliances sitting out on front porches in rural communities throughout the region. Weathered scarecrows and classic Ford Mustangs decorate fields that lie off the beaten path. Many areas of the world claim to have breathtakingly beautiful landscapes, and the Tennessee Valley is no exception. The region has a multitude of rivers which make it popular for fishing, rafting and kayaking. Boating trips and family getaways make the sparkling lakes of the Valley noteworthy, as well. Whether it be Tim's Ford, Guntersville, or one of the area's other scenic lakes, you can find plenty of relaxation – and exhilaration – on the Valley's waters. The Tennessee Valley also has its fair share of underground caves – ranging from Cathedral Caverns in Grant, Alabama, to Raccoon Mountain Caverns in Chattanooga. Stunning vistas can be found as far east as Tennessee's Lookout Mountain, and as far south into the region as Gorham's Bluff, in Pisgah, Alabama.

King Cotton

Cotton fields in the Tennessee Valley are landscapes unquestionably unique to the South. During the fall, many visitors traveling through the area marvel at the seemingly endless white fields of cotton being picked by giant green harvesters. Alabama has long been known as "The Cotton State," with Limestone County recognized as one of the largest cotton-producing counties in the Valley. The term "King Cotton" was frequently used prior to the Civil War to emphasize the economic and political importance of this industry. In the post-Civil War era, cotton became a major currency with which people paid their bills. Sharecroppers and cotton pickers, both black and white, worked the fields from sunrise to sunset, making cotton the sustaining product of the South. Northern "carpet-baggers" and "scalawags" alike recognized the significance that Valley cotton wielded for many years before other agricultural products became viable commercial products. Although ravaged at times by depressions, droughts, floods, and bollweevil infestations, cotton farmers continue this well-respected, long-honored farming tradition. After farmers collect the cotton harvest at the different farms, they transport it to local cotton gins by modular trucks. It is then run through modular feeders to the gin, which separates the cotton from the seed, the latter eventually sold to dairy farmers. The gin bundles the cotton and ships it to regional textile mills. Throughout the entire process, ownership of the cotton usually remains with the farmers. The world market produces between 19 and 21 million bales per year, with the United States contributing about 9 million of those bales.

"There is as much dignity in plowing a field as in writing a poem."
Booker T. Washington

"The cotton industry gets into your blood. In this part of the South, the fall of the year is 'cotton time.'"
H.J. Carter
Owner
North Alabama Gin Company

Kudzu Gone Crazy!

If you do enough traveling in the Tennessee Valley, you'll eventually drive past a rather strange plant named *kudzu*. This large-leafed vine has the capacity to grow 60 feet in a single summer! Kudzu is not commonly known outside the South, nor does it naturally

belong to our region. First introduced at the 1876 Centennial Exposition in Philadelphia, Pennsylvania, it was brought to the South during the Depression by the Soil Conservation Service. The intent was to control erosion and enrich the local barren clay landscape, particularly south of the Tennessee River. Kudzu was planted alongside roads throughout the Valley, and was a source of income for farmers during the 1940s who were compensated by the government for planting it in their fields. Unfortunately, this Asian plant quickly took on a life of its own and started overtaking and often destroying everything in its path. It possesses the ability to rapidly climb the sides of houses, trees, electric poles, and support wires. Rumors that it has kidnapped small children and eaten dogs cannot be substantiated! It is, however, well on its way to becoming the largest non-taxpaying resident of the region, and is justifiably nicknamed as "The Plant that Attacked the Tennessee Valley."

Farmers' Markets

The term "farmers' market" describes a sale in which farmers, growers, or producers from a defined local area sell their produce directly to the public. Unlike roadside markets, which also sell great produce, these markets are fully regulated by the county. Farmers' markets are not necessarily unique to the Tennessee Valley, they're just especially popular in this region. Every part of the country has its own markets with its own unique produce. From the Dutch markets in Pennsylvania where one can smell fresh horseradish being ground, to the outdoor markets in California where one can taste the locally grown herbs and spices, farmers' markets are reflections of an area's

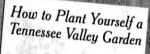

agriculture. Whatever is growing that particular month is what you'll likely find for sale at the market. In addition to the sale of vegetables – many of which can be purchased at most grocery stores – locally made crafts and specialty produce are often available. Unique produce found at farmers' markets within the Valley include pecans, muscadine preserves, gourds, pickled watermelon rinds, pigs' feet, and a wide variety of peppers. Farmers' markets usually smell great and provide opportunities for even the most discriminating of cooks to stock their kitchens with fresh, tasty ingredients.

How to Plant Yourself a Tennessee Valley Garden

Plant four rows of squash:
Squash gossip
Squash indifference
Squash grumbling
Squash selfishness

Plant four rows of lettuce:
Lettuce be faithful
Lettuce be kind
Lettuce be patient
Lettuce really love one another

Plant three rows of peas:
Peas of mind
Peas of heart
Peas of soul

Plant three rows of turnips:
Turnip for meetings
Turnip for service
Turnip to help one another

Plant three rows of thyme:
Thyme for each other
Thyme for family
Thyme for friends

It is guaranteed that at the end of the season, you will reap what you sow!

Gourds Galore

Many visitors to the Valley are often surprised by the high number of gourds found in the area. They are regularly displayed in back yards, craft fairs and farmers' markets. Despite the fact that gourds are inedible, they have become a symbol of the South. Gourds belong to the cucurbitaceae (cucumber) family, and are closely related to squash, melons and pumpkins. People use gourds in a number of ways, from birdhouses, tools, and fishing floats to whistles, rattles, and musical instruments. Although there are approximately 100 genera of gourds, most of them fall into one of three categories: the lagenaria, or hard-shell gourd; the cucurbita, or ornamental gourd; and the luffa, or vegetable sponge. Gourds are tender annuals that thrive in areas where the temperature is between 70 and 85 degrees, and about 100 to 180 days are required for most varieties to mature. Many people prize gourds for their varied shapes, often creating new shapes by tying strings or bands around the gourd when it is young.

Pickin' in the Valley

Not all Valley pickin' involves musical instruments. Name a certain type of fruit or vegetable, and chances are when its season rolls around, there are a number of areas within the region where you can gather some from the tree or vine. Valley residents can pick lettuce in the winter, strawberries in the spring, blueberries and blackberries in the summer, and pumpkins and cotton in the fall. These outdoor activities provide fantastic entertainment for families with little ones. Local newspapers and yellow pages often list which commercial farms allow the general public to go pickin' their own fruits and vegetables. In the fall, you might even locate a hayride or corn maze to try. Such nearby outings are relaxing, inexpensive excuses to get up off the couch and grab some fresh air. For a small fee – usually based on the amount of produce harvested – this can be a fun, enjoyable day outing for the whole family. And, with permission, even the family dog!

The Highs and Lows of Local Weather

Naturally, a primary ingredient for an impressive cottonfield or kudzu wall is an equally impressive dose of hot, Southern sunshine. Tennessee Valley summers have certainly caused more than a few recently-transplanted Northerners to trade in their snow skis for water skis. It is not uncommon for a Tennessee Valley August to consistently average somewhere in the low to mid 90s. Typically, summertime in Tennessee and Alabama boasts higher levels of humidity than other regions of the country. These summertime conditions explain a lot – from our love of iced tea, to the origins of the term "redneck."

On the flip side of that coin is the Tennessee Valley winter season. Although a thick snowfall happens only once every few years, another colorful trait of Tennessee Valley locals is we simply don't deal with snow particularly well. When exploring the Valley in wintertime you need to know about "The Rule." The Rule essentially states that if any radio or TV station reports that more than a handful of snowflakes have fallen to the ground, every school, business, church, and fast-food joint must close for the day. But, being the Tennessee Valley, naturally these advisories do not apply to previously scheduled football games or hunting trips!

One weather characteristic Valley residents would prefer doing without is the infamous Tennessee Valley tornado. When these twisters touch down, they can leave trails of destruction for miles. Consequently, one can find tornado shelters in almost all rural areas within the Valley. Many visitors often mistake these

structures for doghouses or storage sheds. Tornado storm shelters are available in several configurations. Older ones built years ago tend to have concrete block walls with wooden doors. They are usually adjacent to the house or built into the side of a large hill on the property. The second type of structure is usually located a good distance from the house and looks a great deal like the family doghouse. Many of these shelters consist of a concrete, reinforced steel pit and have full ventilation systems. Newer types of weather fortresses are egg-shaped, built of concrete, and completely buried underground. In a regional weather emergency, all three types of shelters will admirably serve the same purpose.

Religion in the Bible Belt's Buckle

The Tennessee Valley is located smack-dab in the middle of America's Bible Belt. You need only look around to see the impact religious culture has had in the Valley area. In certain areas of both Tennessee and Alabama, you can find churches of all denominations in overwhelming numbers. A weekend drive through the countryside can result in visual treasures such as old and beautiful rural churches. With a little research – in the way of newspapers, the Internet, and radio ads – you can easily track down and witness old-fashioned tent revivals and attend gospel "sing-alongs" throughout the year. Because of their citizens' religious beliefs, several counties throughout the Valley prohibit the sale of alcoholic beverages. This is a touchy issue that consistently arises during election time. In addition to the issue of alcohol, the subject of a state lottery raises passionate arguments on both sides as well. Tennessee allows it; Alabama does not. Although surrounded on four sides by states that permit lotteries, Alabama residents continuously veto such gambling activities. There are few things stronger in the South than the religious and moral beliefs of Valley residents.

"I learned more stuff in church than I did in the world."

Reverend Al Green

COUNTRY COMMANDMENTS

1. THERE'S ONLY ONE GOD

2. DON'T WORSHIP THANGS

3. NO CUSS'N

4. GATHER ON THE SABBATH

5. MIND YOUR MA AND PA

6. NO KILL'N

7. NO CHEAT'N

8. DON'T STEAL

9. DON'T LIE

10. NO HANKER'N FOR OTHER'S STUFF

Country Cookin' is Food at its Finest

Anthony Bourdain, author, chef, and host of the Travel Channel's *No Reservations* once stated, "Traveling and eating are about letting things happen." What a great viewpoint! Cuisine is very close to the hearts of Southerners. Perhaps *too* close, with Alabama and Tennessee ranking numbers one and nine, respectively, on the list of America's most obese states (although locals prefer the term "prosperous"). What is the silver lining to this cloud? It's that our food tastes downright delicious! Sitting down to eat is also a hugely popular social activity in this region. In the Tennessee Valley, residents go to a restaurant as much to visit their friends and neighbors as they do to eat. These factors contribute to our region occasionally being referred to as the Stroke Belt. Indeed, it could be argued that Tennessee Valley cooking often hinges upon all of the wrong foods.

"It is a scientific fact that your body will not absorb cholesterol if you take it from another person's plate."
Dave Barry
Syndicated Columnist

If you'd like to experience a typical Southern breakfast make sure you bring your appetite. This breakfast will traditionally include eggs accompanied by a slab of ham the size of a small dog. Grits and biscuits often complement this plate along with two different types of gravy and plenty of butter. It is almost guaranteed you will not leave a Southern breakfast table hungry. Unlike up North, folks usually eat lunch – often referred to by old-timers as "dinner" – fairly early. This meal, which usually equals the amount of food eaten on a daily basis by 98 percent of the world's population, generally starts out with a tall glass of iced tea. Unless you object, the tea will almost always be sweet. Any sweet tea served will probably come with enough sugar in it to cause you difficulty getting the plastic spoon to the bottom of the glass. Also, hot tea is a rarity in these parts. If you request a "Coke" from a true Valley waitress, you will often be asked "What kind?" At which point you must specify whether you are in the mood for Dr. Pepper, Coca-Cola, Pepsi, Sprite, etc. Other than tea, most non-alcoholic beverages served in old-fashioned restaurants are referred to as "cokes."

You can also experience true Southern restaurants featuring numerous "blue-plate" specials. These specials typically consist of a selection of meats and vegetables which have failed to make the list of Weight Watchers' acceptable diet foods. The dishes are almost always as rich in cholesterol as they are in taste. Depending on the day of the week, the blue-plate special entrée will usually be a choice of Southern-fried chicken, country-fried steak, fried ham, or fried fish. A basket of fried hush puppies will often accompany the entrée. The side vegetable selection will include French fries, fried okra, fried green tomatoes, fried squash, and possibly deep fried pickles. For dessert, do not be surprised to find a sweet, fried fruit pie.

Astute readers might detect a note of similarity concerning how these Southern dishes are prepared! Believe it or not, there is a historical explanation behind the Tennessee Valley's love of fried foods. Tradition has it that during the hot summer months, the cooks in the kitchen would prefer frying the majority of foods served because it was quicker than other methods such as baking. This enabled the field hands to eat quickly and promptly return to their duties. Additionally, frying didn't heat up the house, which as anyone who has lived through a Valley summer can tell you is a big plus! Frying was relatively inexpensive because lard was plentiful and cast iron skillets were cheap. These combined circumstances resulted in a cooking tradition that to this day symbolizes the best and the worst of the Valley's culinary habits.

Grits

Any discussion of Tennessee Valley cooking must include an entire paragraph on grits. For at least 400 years, this dish, nicknamed "The Southern Oatmeal," has been an integral part of the traditional Southern diet. According to history books, in 1607 the colonists of Jamestown, Virginia, were greeted by cordial Native Americans offering a dish they called "rockahominie." This maize-based dish, salted and seasoned with animal fat, is known today as grits. Grits have been a particularly successful meal in the South because of their resilience in times of extreme heat and humidity. Because it was both affordable and abundant, the food helped many Southerners survive the Great Depression of the 1930s. Grits are a fairly uncomplicated dish, and now store-bought brands come in all manner of flavors, from bacon to ham and cheese. Instant grits can be made in under a minute, although any self-respecting Southern cook will insist on spending at least 15 minutes to prepare them in the traditional manner. Inventive regional connoisseurs have added butter, salt, pepper, cheese, garlic, and countless other ingredients to grits over the years, but the basics remain unchanged; grits come from milled corn kernels. Cooks steam and split the grains, and remove the smaller granules. Grits are usually added to a pot of boiling water, though many prefer to bake their grits. Although grits themselves have no fat or cholesterol, once a local has served you some, it is a safe bet there will be a huge pat of butter melting on top!

"What the heck's a grit?"

Karen Heslin
New Jersey Transplant

Catfish, Hush Puppies, and More Catfish

Stories are passed down from Southern grandparents about them. Stories about how putting your hand in the right pool of water, and wiggling your fingers would result in catching one for dinner that evening. Stories about the monster that almost ate Great-Grandpa Winston when he was a teenager! These stories, of course, are about the South's beloved catfish. In every medium-sized Tennessee Valley city, it seems there is at least one local restaurant known solely for its ability to cook 'em up. Alabama is second in the nation for catfish consumption, while Chattanooga's Tennessee Aquarium regularly recognizes National Catfish Month every August. Catfish have occasionally even been spotted on grills at Valley barbeque competitions. Magnificent recipes and methods abound for baked, grilled, and pan-broiled catfish, but the local preference is, naturally, to fry it. Prior to dropping the fish into the deep-fryer or frying pan, local chefs typically roll and coat the uncooked fish with a good cornmeal and seasoning salt mixture. When the crispy fish (either whole or filleted) is placed on a plate, it is usually accompanied by tartar sauce, lemons, slaw (that's *coleslaw* to visitors from north of the Mason-Dixon line), and hush puppies. Hush puppies, of course, are simply little balls of fried, seasoned cornbread which always accompany the catfish in these parts.

Barbeque – The South's Answer to French Cuisine

Many people who aren't all too familiar with barbequing techniques believe barbeque (also known as BBQ), prepared and served in many areas of the United States, is a one-dimensional process in which the end product is somewhat reminiscent of an old-fashioned "Sloppy Joe." For those in the know, however, the mention of barbequing immediately brings to mind images of wood smoke, dawn-to-dusk cooking rituals, cleavers on wooden blocks, multitudes of sauces, and closely guarded secret family recipes. Barbequing is not unique to either the Valley or the Deep South. With ample justification, many believe the best barbeque comes from North Carolina. Lexington, North Carolina even proclaims it is the "Barbeque Capital of the World." Other states, such as Texas and Kansas, also lay claim to this culinary honor. In Tennessee, Memphis residents insist their city, with more than 100 restaurants specializing in pork and ribs, is the undisputed champion in the preparation of this delicacy. When all is said and done, however, it usually depends upon the types of meats, sauces, and preparations Southerners have grown up with that determines their preferred selection. One thing is certain – Southerners love their barbeque.

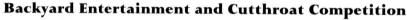

Backyard Entertainment and Cutthroat Competition

Some could argue that barbeque is society's great equalizer. It cuts through social stratums and appeals to society at all levels. Once served exclusively in homes, it has since moved to many types of commercial establishments, such as restaurants, catering services, joints, dives, and makeshift drive-thrus. It is served at weddings and sports events and is lovingly prepared in the backyards of millions of homes throughout the nation. Grills for barbequing can be as diverse as the types of meats they serve up. With beer in hand, many backyard connoisseurs spend hours preparing this tasty delight using a variety of methods. Barbeque chefs' cooking set-ups range from the family's traditional Weber grill, to cinder blocks, old refrigerators, or shoveled-out holes in the ground. If you visit a large barbeque competition, you are likely to wander upon a *professional grillmaster*. These hard-core experts proudly cook on a variety of grills – which can be so expensive they require home-equity loans!

Barbeque festivals are held in middle Tennessee and north Alabama throughout the year. Tennessee is host to one of the most famous international barbequing events – Lynchburg's Jack Daniel's World Championship Invitational Barbeque. In Alabama, you can visit Decatur's Riverfest Alabama State Championship or Huntsville's Whistle Stop Festival and Rocket City BBQ Cook-Off. The larger contests are usually held under the auspices of either the Kansas City Barbeque Society or Memphis Barbequing Association. During these competitions, contestants often sleep in tents or campers near their cooking set-ups, enabling them to regulate the grill and oven temperatures. The contestants either drive or tow their rigs to barbeque cook-offs in pursuit of money, prizes, or simply culinary recognition. With all of that comes the inevitable social comradery between the contestants and the public. In addition to delicious food and the excuse to knock back a few beers, a great amount of old-fashioned social bonding occurs at these multi-day events. Win, lose, or draw – these dedicated chefs have fun pursuing this traditional Southern pastime!

Cooking and Ordering Barbeque in the South

Throughout the South and Southwest, barbequing has become not only a tradition but a way of life. Preparation of pork shoulders often starts the night before and involves a variety of "pits" using wood fires or charcoal to cook the meats. There are many decisions to be made along the way concerning both the cooking and the ordering of barbeque. In regards to its preparation, if the cooks prefer the traditional use of wood to charcoal or gas, they will all have their own opinions concerning the type of wood to use, whether it be hickory, oak, mesquite, or apple. A good barbeque restaurant in the South can be recognized not only by the number of cars in its parking lot, but also by the amount of wood stacked behind the building. Regardless of the type of fuel used, one key secret to good barbequing is time. Cook it slow and steady! Barbeque experts recommend keeping the food moist throughout the process. A good pit-master never rushes the preparation of this delicacy. He or she may prefer to let the meat simmer, adding nothing to it, or possibly use a dry rub or baste with a secret marinade. Sauces of all types can be found on barbeque today. Vinegar, pepper, tomato sauce, apple juice, and beer are just a few of the most popular sauce bases. Backyard chefs may use a simple paintbrush to apply a baste, while commercial restaurants have been known to apply large amounts of sauce with none other than mops! As with the cook, the customer also has serious choices to make. Ordering barbeque in the South and Southwest involves a complicated series of decisions, which must be thoroughly considered and discussed before you place your order. These decisions often include one or more of the following choices: Pork, beef brisket, ribs, or chicken? Sandwich or plate combo? Inside or outside cuts? Pulled or chopped meat? Table sauces – tomato base, vinegar base, hot sauce, or white sauce? Side dish? (Side dishes are traditionally baked beans – often with a hint of sorghum, molasses, brown sugar, or green pepper – and slaw using either a vinegar or mayonnaise base.) And, when in the Deep South, don't be surprised to find a big slice of onion or pickle served up on the side. Bon appetit!

"Above all, have fun! Remember, barbecue isn't brain surgery."

Steven Raichlen
The Barbecue! Bible

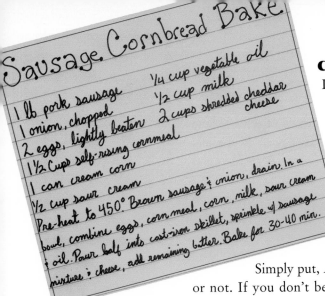

Sausage Cornbread Bake

1 lb pork sausage
1 onion, chopped
2 eggs, lightly beaten
1½ Cups self-rising cornmeal
1 can cream corn
½ cup sour cream
¼ cup vegetable oil
½ cup milk
2 cups shredded cheddar cheese

Pre-heat to 450°. Brown sausage & onion, drain. In a bowl, combine eggs, corn meal, corn, milk, sour cream & oil. Pour half into cast-iron skillet, sprinkle w/ sausage mixture & cheese, add remaining batter. Bake for 30-40 min.

Cornbread

Long before Plymouth Rock, Native Americans were drying and grinding corn into meal, the primary ingredient in cornbread. Throw in a cast iron skillet, a little grease, a few eggs, and some cornmeal, and you have one of the South's most distinguished dishes. Influence from other areas of the country has brought forth varieties with ingredients such as jalapeños, sour cream, and olives. Cornbread variations can range from cornbread fritters to cornbread pizza dough and cornbread pudding. But make no mistake – cornbread can be a hot, controversial issue in these parts! Simply put, Americans are divided on whether cornbread is made with sugar or not. If you don't believe it, ask the oldest Southern woman you know, and brace yourself for an emotional response! Typically, your average Tennessee Valley chef will insist that no sugar whatsoever be mixed into the cornbread. There are, of course, exceptions to every rule – but most Northern cornbread recipes have sugar, and most Southern recipes do not. The country is even divided on the spelling (it is spelled with two words in the rest of the country, but rest assured *we* are the enlightened ones). In fact, one of our very own Valley cities, South Pittsburgh, Tennessee, hosts the National Cornbread Festival every spring.

"The idea that one can consume too much cornbread is a myth perpetrated by corn-haters and small-minded bureaucrats."

Jeremy Jackson
The Cornbread Book

Fried Green What?

Some people hear the term "fried green tomatoes" and think of the Hollywood movie bearing the same name. Around these parts, fried green tomatoes are not such a peculiar novelty. When folks from the Deep South think upon this subject, thoughts often turn to country-style cooking and a lot of kitchen-table talk. This may not be high-class cuisine, but it is undeniably good! The Southern tradition of frying less-than-ripe tomatoes (as well as preparing other delights such as grits, collard greens, and cornbread) is not always simply a culinary activity. For some, it is a way of life, handed down from generation to generation. The recipe for fried green tomatoes is very adaptable – some folks prefer using cornmeal over flour, others want ranch dressing or a bit of garlic to embellish the taste. Whichever way you prepare this old-time favorite, remember, it's generally not the food, but the companionship that counts!

"The old-fashioned country way to cook fried green tomatoes (they really don't have to be totally green) is to slice them thin, add a little salt, dip in meal, and fry quickly in fat or oil. And for heaven's sake, don't use a heavy batter. Delicious."

Sue Dawson
Former Home Economics Teacher

FRANNY'S FRIED GREEN TOMATOES

1 EGG BEATEN
1 CUP MILK (BUTTERMILK IS OK)
1 CUP RISING FLOUR
½ CUP CORNMEAL
½ TSP. SALT
6-8 GREEN TOMATOES (CUT INTO 1/4' SLICES)
BACON DRIPPINGS OR VEGETABLE OIL

MIX EGG AND MILK/BUTTERMILK IN A SHALLOW DISH. WORKING IN BATCHES, DIP TOMATO SLICES INTO THE EGG MIXTURE, ALLOWING EXCESS TO DRIP BACK INTO DISH. COAT WITH FLOUR MIXTURE. FRY IN HOT OIL (375) IN A LARGE HEAVY SKILLET UNTIL BROWNED, TURNING ONCE WITH TONGS. TRANSFER TO DRAIN.
YIELD: 6 SERVINGS.

Shine From the Mountain

You might not know who he is, but it's a safe bet that through only a few degrees of separation, you're connected to a bonafide moonshiner. Moonshine is a distinctly Southern drink – with a uniquely powerful kick. The word "moonshine" stems from the nocturnal nature of the distilling process. It needs to be made under cover of darkness, because as any *Dukes of Hazzard* fan can tell you, moonshine is as illegal as it can be. In fact, the history of NASCAR is rooted in the shine runners' necessity for high-speed engines! Owners of moonshine stills pay dearly when caught. Stills are usually found in secluded areas, due to the fact that distillation requires heat to boil the alcoholic liquor from the mash, which produces plenty of visible steam.

"Well, between Scotch and nothin', I suppose I'd take Scotch. It's the nearest thing to good moonshine I can find."
William Faulkner

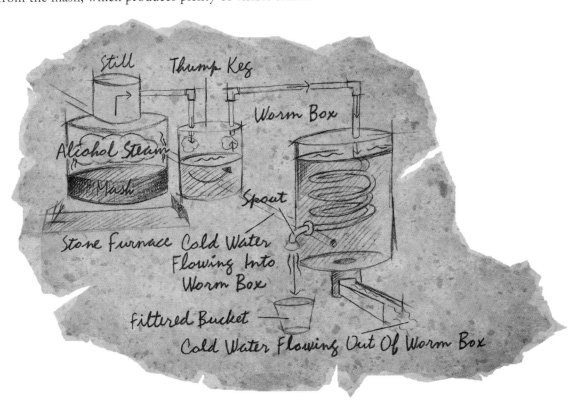

Moonshine has a slew of nicknames, some of which include White Lightning, Mule-Kick, Rotgut, Bathtub Gin, Stumpholewater, and as "the original" Mountain Dew. Its origins are uncomplicated – southern brewers who either didn't wish to pay taxes on alcohol or weren't allowed to make alcohol due to prohibition or local legislation, took matters into their own hands. With a still, which is a fairly simple contraption, moonshiners take ground corn, soak it in hot water, and add yeast, thus beginning the fermentation process. After heating, evaporating, and condensing, the result is a very fiery, very illegal batch of moonshine.

One fundamental difference between moonshine and store-bought whiskey is the aging process. When moonshine comes out of the still, it is bottled as a clear liquid. When you find a bottle of Wild Turkey or Jack Daniel's in a store, it has a golden-amber color to it. This is attributed to the liquid being aged in oak barrels for years, which, thankfully, also takes away the harsh taste. Another difference is that moonshine's lack of government involvement allows for impurities and dangerously high alcohol levels. Thousands of people have died from poisoned alcohol. But regardless of its taste, contraband status, and nonadherance to FDA standards, chances are there is someone in your county drinking some moonshine right now!

"It don't take a genius to make it."
Carl Cantrell
Former Tennessee Moonshiner
(AP news release)

Valley Music

It is said that music can serve as an acoustical time machine, temporarily transporting people away from their everyday problems. The music most typically associated with the Tennessee Valley is, naturally, country. However, it should be noted that this region is also rich with authentic bluegrass, rockabilly, gospel, blues, rock'n'roll, and zydeco music. The instruments of the Valley are as varied as the sounds they produce. In addition to the guitar, other Southern instruments include the autoharp, stand-up bass, harmonica, mandolin, banjo, dobro, dulcimer, fiddle, ukulele, and washboard.

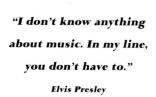

"I don't know anything about music. In my line, you don't have to."

Elvis Presley

There are plenty of musical events in this neck of the woods, and your only challenge might be tracking down the particular type of music you prefer. While the larger events are well advertised months in advance, the smaller, unknown – and often unscheduled – performances provide some of the Valley's finest music. Your best bet is to review the local newspapers, then hit the highways and hard-to-find, back-country roads. Many nonmusical festivals in the area have unannounced, impromptu jams. And simply stopping to ask for directions can lead to you thoroughly enjoying countless hours of music at an unscheduled stop. If you're up for a truly unique musical experience, check out some local "buck dancing," which often accompanies the playing of bluegrass music. Some onlookers might liken this type of dancing to someone trying to stomp roaches, but it certainly provides plenty of fun for all involved! Those with a good pair of cowboy boots are always encouraged to pull 'em on and take a stab at line dancing to some good rockin' country, whilst the occasional zydeco performance – complete with washboards – can compel even the stodgiest of killjoys to flash a grin and do a twirl.

The Valley's love of music has certainly been recognized by outsiders. Muscle Shoals has recorded some of the greatest musicians in history, from Bob Dylan to The Rolling Stones to Aretha Franklin. Black Southern gospel, with its bittersweet history rooted deep in the days of slavery, has spread its way from forbidden spiritual country sing-alongs to world-famous R&B-chart-topping singles. Nashville is known the world over as Music City, U.S.A., and hosts the mammoth Country Music Association (CMA) festival, which regularly draws capacity crowds. Right down the road, Manchester, Tennessee, serves as playground to Bonnaroo, a yearly music festival that now draws more than 90,000 visitors in a single weekend. Huntsville has its impressive, three-day Big Spring Jam, while Chattanooga hosts the spectacular Riverfest. Athens, Alabama, has a jewel of a festival in its Old Time Fiddlers' Convention, and the splendid sounds of blues and jazz echo throughout Florence when the W.C. Handy Music Festival comes to town every summer. Of course, the enjoyment of music does not hinge upon historical significance, large festivals, or an area's reputation. It requires only two things – good music and good fans. The music awaits – so get out there and start those feet a-tappin'!

"Country music to me is heartfelt music that speaks to the common man. It is about real-life stories with rather simple melodies that the average person can follow. Country music should speak directly and simply about the highs and lows of life. Something that anyone can relate to."

George Jones

Our Love of School Sports

If there is anything that the folks in this region can claim to love as much as cooking or music, it is football. Fall weekends in the Valley usually start off with a little "Friday night fever," where communities come out to support their local high school football teams. On Saurdays, the region virtually shuts down when the University of Tennessee's Volunteers, the University of Alabama's Crimson Tide, or Auburn University's Tigers gear up for kick-off. Vanderbilt fans are no less enthusiastic, and the same holds true for supporters of Alabama A&M, Middle Tennessee State University, and the University of North Alabama. The rivalry surrounding the Iron Bowl (Alabama vs. Auburn) draws millions of emotional fans to television sets across the state, regardless of the teams' individual season records going into the game. The University of Tennessee's Neyland Stadium is the largest stadium in the South, with attendance averaging more than 100,000 visitors a game! Hordes of RVs with grills, speakers, and lawn chairs in tow begin filing into campuses well before actual gameday. Tailgating parties are beloved here, and can pull in plenty of cheering,

"Watching the games weekly in the fall is like a ritual, and all activity must be scheduled around them. Having a son graduate from Auburn and one at Alabama, we are now a very mixed family."

John Emerson
Ardent University of Tennessee Fan

burger-eating fans. This support extends to other sports as well, especially basketball and baseball. The University of Tennessee's Lady Volunteers basketball team commands a fanatical following, having pocketed more than half a dozen national championships in the past two decades. But for now, football reigns supreme. Ask most children in the region which SEC team is the best, and their parental guidance and training will most likely bring forth a quick, passionate response!

"The price of victory is high, but so are the rewards."

Paul "Bear" Bryant
Head Coach
University of Alabama (1958 – 1982)

Outdoor Sports

Given the spectacular natural surroundings and the number of state and federal parks we have in the Tennessee Valley, it is not surprising the region offers a bountiful supply of outdoor sporting activities. Canoeing, kayaking, fishing, boating, camping, hunting, and hiking associations are in good supply. In recent years, geocaching has even spread into the area. For the less athletically inclined, there are bird-watching groups, and for the more sporting types, climbing and mountain biking opportunities exist as well. And for all you thrill seekers, the Tennessee Valley even offers up a healthy dose of both hang gliding and skydiving.

Paddling 'Round the Year

Canoeing is one year-round outdoor activity many folks often overlook when searching for something different to do on a weekend. This sport can provide an inexpensive outing, which, depending upon the ages of the children, an entire family can enjoy. Regardless of your preference to canoe on a lake, creek, stream, or river, the Tennessee Valley can provide the setting. Kayak and canoe trips on rivers run from easy (Class I) to difficult (Class V) and provide a myriad of experiences and beautiful scenes. In middle Tennessee, many canoe enthusiasts visit Tim's Ford Lake, Normandy Lake, the Elk River, and the Duck River. In north Alabama, you should consider canoeing the Flint River or the Sipsey River, located in the historic Bankhead National Forest. All of these rivers provide beautiful scenery and easy Class I and II runs. If interested in swamp-paddling to view wildlife, readers are encouraged to try the Wheeler National Wildlife Refuge east of Decatur, Alabama. Seasoned paddlers looking for more difficult rivers in Alabama should consider Town Creek River on Sand Mountain, and Little River in Little River Canyon.

"At our entrance we have a sign that says 'You are now entering a stress-free zone.' After a day on the river, you understand the reason for the sign."

Ben Towry
Owner
Elk River Canoe Rental

Watersports and Boating

The silver lining to the blistering hot summers we experience here in the South is that we have a great excuse to get out and play in our lakes and rivers. Boating, water-skiing, wakeboarding, jet-skiing, and tubing are all in full swing when summer rolls around each year. On a nice sunny day, Tim's Ford or Guntersville Lake will be covered with recreational boaters and water-loving partiers. It seems that every stretch of shoreline has a fairly respectable cliff, featuring a rope swing from which the young-at-heart perform "can-openers" and "cannonballs" until the sun goes down. The Tennessee Valley has a slew of boating, sailing, and skiing clubs that allow non-boat-owners to get in on the action if they play their cards right. Festivals held on the riverbanks of Decatur, Florence, Nashville, Chattanooga, and many other major Southern cities always manage to attract visitors arriving by boat.

Local Hunting and Fishing

Hunting opportunities abound in this part of the Southeast. Both Tennessee and Alabama have established excellent wildlife management areas with impressive amounts of acreage. Depending on the season, hunters pursue deer, turkey, quail, dove, and waterfowl with shotguns, rifles, and bows. Fishing is equally popular in this part of the country. Whether you'd like to spend a quiet afternoon alone by a riverbank, enjoy quality time on the lake with your family, or simply take in the serene beauty of a mountain stream or wetland, the Tennessee Valley provides a variety of locations prime for freshwater fishing. If you have a competitive spirit, the region hosts numerous fishing tournaments throughout the year, particularly along the TVA lakes and reservoirs of north Alabama. Many of these are high-dollar tournaments (Bassmasters, BASS, FLW, Red Man, etc.), held year round, and host some of the nation's top anglers using the best rigs available. Be it striped, largemouth or smallmouth bass, catfish, walleye, bluegill, or crappie, the Valley offers some of the best fishing in the Southeast.

"Never go snipe-hunting twice."
Southern Expression

Hiking and Camping

Tennessee and Alabama have some remarkably scenic state parks. Visiting these is a must for Tennessee Valley inhabitants. Whether you take a quick day-hike or a week-long camping trip, the green forests, spectacular waterfalls, and lush canyons of the area are sure to satisfy. On occasion, you will stumble across ancient Native American carvings etched into rock. Perhaps it's the fleeting glance of a family of white-tailed deer that provides the highlight of your trip, or a moment of total serenity only reachable when sitting miles deep inside a forest. These fantastic experiences are not exclusive only to Eagle Scouts and wilderness experts! The Tennessee and Alabama state park authorities have gone to great lengths to make the parks as safe as possible for even the most naive of couch potatoes. This book features overviews of many parks, canyons, and hiking trails ideal for family weekend outings. You are encouraged to grab a trusted pair of hiking boots and visit each of these natural beauties at your leisure.

"Alabama has the American golfer's equivalent of Disney World."

**Golf Magazine,
on the Robert Trent
Jones Golf Trail**

Golf

Due to its climate and terrain, some of the greatest and most affordable golf in the world can be found right here in the Tennessee Valley. Local weather affords golfers opportunities to play the courses twelve months a year. Rolling mountains, countrysides, lakes, and reservoirs provide perfect settings for the many golf courses within the region. In addition to numerous private courses, both states proudly feature nationally-recognized public courses, many of which are built alongside state parks. The Robert Trent Jones (RTJ) Golf Trail initially placed Alabama squarely on the national golfing map. There are nine RTJ facilities in the state, four of which fall within this book's area of concentration. *The New York Times* calls the RTJ Golf Trail "some of the best public golf on earth." Tennessee's answer to the RTJ Golf Trail are the highly respected and beautiful Bear Trace Courses. These Jack Nicklaus-designed courses are picturesque, playable, and challenging. Four of the five are built alongside state parks. These, in addition to other beautiful public and private courses within the Valley, should not be overlooked and are splendid additions to the Tennessee Valley's list of geographical assets.

"The only time my prayers are never answered is on the golf course."

**Billy Graham
Southern Evangelist**

Outhouses and Other Classy Subjects

In wrapping up our description of what constitutes the meat-and-potatoes of the Tennessee Valley's character, we are also forced to acknowledge some of its less glamorous traits. But just as every cloud has a silver lining, every off-kilter oddity has its own "something." Every weathered old ramshackle barn has its history; every engineless Camaro sitting up on blocks has its potential. As we delve deeper into the personality of the region, four final, colorful, subjects entertainingly join our list: outhouses, yard sales, boiled peanuts, and fashionably-challenged inhabitants.

Old Outhouses

Notwithstanding what your interests are in touring the Valley, any writer would be remiss if he or she failed to describe one of the most important subjects concerning

weekend travelers – restroom facilities. Although tourists in the Valley regularly joke about the use of "one-holer" outhouses, those of you who make a habit of straying far enough from the beaten path will occasionally confront a variety of uniquely configured bathrooms and toilets. When adventuring in the Deep South, you may face such challenges as pulling rusted release-chains, using non-functioning electric eyes, or working stuck handles. Actual outhouses are few and far between these days (thankfully), but rest assured – they are still out there!

The Southern Yard Sale

In this region of the South, it often seems that between Friday night and Saturday morning at least 10,000 instant businesses mysteriously arise from the ground like worms on a wet sidewalk. Travel down any Tennessee Valley back road and you will probably spot a bonafide Southern yard sale. They can be found in parking lots, front yards, under trees, in garages, outside schools and churches, and sometimes simply set up along the roadside. Contrary to public opinion, many of these are not small sales endeavors where Mom and Dad stand in front of their bungalow, holding hands and selling items they truly regret parting with. In reality, some of these local yard sales are so large the vendors bring in portable toilets, elect mayors, and apply for zoning code variances. The old saying, "buy in haste, repent in leisure," unquestionably applies to yard sales. People tend to buy – and sell – just about anything in these parts. Be it trash or treasure, if the prospective item can be dragged out of the house, garage, or woods, it can be sold or traded before noon. Everything from worn, tattered t-shirts and broken dishes to valuable antiques constitute fair game at a yard sale. Most folks attending these functions don't realize they are often competing against professional scavengers and cutthroat bargain hunters. Many of these highly trained shoppers travel as "tag-teams" with marked-up maps and newspaper clippings. They arrive at the sales long before they are even scheduled to begin, pick out the best stuff, often use the host's bathroom, and are on their way to their next heist as quickly as possible. The yard sale experience can be an enjoyable one, and a place to meet some friendly new people – even if they are competing for your newly-found treasures.

Seriously Now, Boiled Peanuts?

Whether you like them or not, boiled peanuts, like collard and mustard greens, are a specialty of the South. Sometimes referred to as "country caviar," this unique food can be found at festivals, out-of-the-way gas stations, and even roadside stands. Cooked slowly for hours in salty water, they have a unique texture and taste. The two types typically sold in the Valley are *cajun* and *regular*. While many think that boiled peanuts resemble stale, wilted lima beans, to the select few, they are the best thing since sliced bread!

Bobby Ray Doesn't Wear Gucci

And finally, we come to our final unglamorous issue – the rather humorous subject of the occasional fashionably challenged Southerner. Along with the Tennessee Valley's somewhat laid-back pace of life, comes, from time to time, an extremely laid-back approach to appearances. While there are millions of well-dressed, well-groomed locals, the undeniable fact remains that a collection of scruffy-looking, tank-top-wearing good ol' boys and girls also add spice to our scenery. Worn-out ballcaps (usually displaying logos for either a state university or a tractor company) are quite popular in the region. Oftentimes, restaurant patrons can be seen eating with their caps on at the table. You may also notice round indentations in the back pocket of blue jeans, impressed over time by cans of chewing tobacco. Are these characters especially glamorous? Not really, but they're a colorful addition to the scenery of the Tennessee Valley nonetheless.

In a Boiled Nutshell

The Tennessee Valley's personality is one of a kind. It has been molded by a unique economic, political, and military history, and has emerged as the place we love to call home. The food, pastimes, music, and idiosyncrasies can often be found, in some form, in other parts of the country. But just as you might hesitate purchasing recordings by a New Jersey-based bluegrass group, or think twice before ordering country-fried steak off the menu of a Seattle restaurant, we should smile at the fact that different people in far away places appreciate what we are all about. And with good reason!

> *"The eating of boiled peanuts is an acquired taste. You have to eat them while drinking scotch."*
>
> **Bill Vosahlik**
> **Huntsville, Alabama**

The next four chapters provide you with a look at some of what the Tennessee Valley has to offer regarding unique entertainment and travel. Remember, reading about these opportunities is only the first step. Go on some trips and see for yourself what makes our area so great. At the end of this book, an appendix with contact information is provided to assist you in your travel planning. For the time being, however, make up a big pitcher of iced tea, grab some boiled peanuts, and start reading!

CHAPTER V:
Tennessee Attractions and Locations Within the Valley
The Volunteer State

The origin of Tennessee's unique nickname stems from a group of soldiers during the War of 1812. Serving under General Andrew Jackson, these volunteer soldiers from Tennessee displayed such remarkable valor, they ended up having their entire home state labeled in their honor. But perhaps even closer to the hearts of SEC sports fans is the fact that the state's biggest university adopted the name as well.

Sports are a big deal in Tennessee, and if you are lucky enough to catch a Volunteers game, (whether it be football, basketball, or baseball) the experience is definitely an exciting one. College sports are not all that Tennessee has to offer. Unlike Alabama, Tennessee boasts an NBA basketball team, an NFL football team, and an NHL hockey team.

If sports just aren't your bag, fear not, for the Volunteer State boasts a multitude of other activities. From Opryland to Graceland, Tennessee has served as the backbone of some of the country's best music. Nashville is home to the Country Music Hall of Fame and Museum, and Chattanooga's Riverbend Festival regularly offers such high-caliber musical performances that it draws more than half a million visitors each year.

The nature and landscape of this state offer a multitude of activities for those who love the outdoors. If you are in the mood for a great hike, check out the Cumberland Trail or the Old Stone Fort State Park in Manchester. Plenty of river-based entertainment awaits you as well – whether it be a casual trip down the Tennessee on a riverboat or a kayaking adventure off of the Natchez Trace. If you're a thrill seeker, you can get your fill of heart-pounding excitement by hang gliding off of Lookout Mountain. Tennessee has top-notch aquariums with bizarre fish, zoos with exotic creatures, and perhaps strangest of all, dry counties with world-famous whiskey distilleries. Indeed, the excuse "there's nothing to do around here" holds no water in these parts.

History buffs have got it made in the state of Tennessee. You can find historic homes, buildings, and museums throughout the state. The Civil War definitely left its mark on Tennessee, and artifacts and stories can be found throughout the region. Chattanooga is home to the African-American Museum, and you can discover some good history lessons at the Tennessee River Museum as well.

This chapter provides just a glimpse of the Tennessee Valley attractions that are available for exploration. Enjoy!

Tennessee at a Glance

Statehood Admission:	June 1, 1796
State Bird:	Mockingbird
State Flower:	Iris
State Tree:	Yellow poplar
Area:	42,146 sq. mi. (36th in U.S.)
Land:	41,220 sq. mi. (34th in U.S.)
Water:	926 sq. mi. (32nd in U.S.)
Agriculture:	Soybeans, cotton, tobacco, livestock and livestock products, dairy products, cattle, hogs
Industry:	Chemicals, transportation equipment, rubber, plastics
Geographic Center:	5 miles northeast of Murfreesboro
Population:	5,841,748
Persons per sq. mile:	138.0
State Name Origin:	Named after Cherokee Indian villages called "Tanasi"

"In the South, the breeze blows softer ...
neighbors are friendlier, nosier, and more talkative.
(By contrast with the Yankee, the Southerner never uses one word
when ten or twenty will do) ... This is a different place.
Our way of thinking is different, as are our ways of seeing,
laughing, singing, eating, meeting, and parting. Nothing about us is
quite the same as in the country to the north and west."

Charles Kuralt
Southerners: Portrait of a People

Introduction to Middle and Southeast Tennessee
Where History Meets Beauty

"Tennessee" has its roots in an Indian word, "Tanasi," meaning "meeting place at the waters." Starting with the Cumberland River in Nashville, then heading south down both boundaries of the Tennessee River, there is history and beauty galore. Most folks know about Nashville's musical attractions, museums, and historical icons. Names such as Andrew Jackson and David Crockett are at once associated with this part of the state. In southeast Tennessee, both visitors and residents are generally knowledgeable about Chattanooga's many tourist attractions, which have developed along the river. But there is much more to middle and southeast Tennessee than the bright lights of the well known large cities.

"Except for the East Coast, I cannot think of any place that has more of America's history woven through its story. The expanding frontier, the age of Jackson, the Civil War, the Great Depression, the New Deal, two world wars, the struggle for civil rights – Middle Tennessee played key roles in all of them. The Middle Tennessee landscape offers much to write about, too. The scenery may not inspire awe, but it is beautiful. It is intimate. It can be taken in and loved. And it is much more diverse than many people realize, ranging from the mountains of the Cumberland Plateau to the swampy bottoms along the Tennessee River. In between are dense forests, rolling bluegrass pastures, and some of America's most lovely rivers."

Robert Brandt
Touring the Middle Tennessee Backroads

From Nashville south to the Alabama state line lies a beautiful area that must not be missed. Although those of you who have explored it know the region is physically pristine, the rest will be pleasantly surprised when you learn about the multitude of cultural attractions that await you. The Civil War ravaged middle Tennessee, but well-manicured battlefields, parks, and war memorial trails are preserved for future generations. Rolling hills, horse farms, antebellum homes, and back-road antique shops are just over the next hill. If you're interested in visiting the whiskey distilleries Tennessee is known for, the world-famous George Dickel and Jack Daniel distilleries are only a scenic afternoon's drive away. Those interested in touring state-of-the-art industrial facilities must make plans to visit the modern Nissan manufacturing plant in Murfreesboro or the Saturn plant in Spring Hill.

An exploratory trip along Route 64 in the southern part of the region provides a leisurely journey into the more off-beaten areas. This route skirts the bottom of the state through 10 counties and takes you through such delightful areas as Winchester, Fayetteville, Pulaski, Lawrenceburg, and even crosses the Natchez Trace Parkway. If you are interested in outdoor activities or just plain sightseeing, you simply can't go wrong with middle Tennessee. Camping, fishing, mountain biking, and kayaking are all available around the area's numerous rivers, reservoirs, lakes, and various state parks. If you wish to venture out and learn about middle Tennessee, you are sure to be pleasantly surprised.

Introduction to Nashville
Music City, U.S.A.

When most people think of Memphis, images of the Mississippi River, Elvis, barbeque, blues music, and the Civil War immediately come to mind. When people think of Nashville, country music generally springs to mind. An attempt to list all of the musical events in this beautiful city would be fruitless – there are simply too many of them. Whatever your favorite type of music, you can find it here. Few other cities in the country showcase the quality, quantity, and diverse styles of music found in Nashville.

Nashville provides visitors and locals with a wide variety of options that extend beyond the downtown area. Its rivers, mountains, tradition, and history represent all things Southern. If you've never visited Nashville, it is an experience not to be missed.

"Nashville offers music anytime, of any kind, anywhere, fifty-two weekends a year. When you want to get away and you want an authentic experience, Music City is the perfect escape."

Butch Spyridon
President
Nashville Area
Convention and Visitors Bureau

If you want to expand your horizons beyond the "homes of the stars" tours, Music Valley Drive, and Broadway Street's honky tonks, there exists a world of attractions and points of interest that appeal to locals and tourists alike. You need only to stop by the visitor center to pick up brochures and a walking tour map. These will help you identify the many unique sites that have made Nashville the popular city it is today. The visitor center offers a free walking tour map of cultural centers, historical enclaves, and beautiful Gothic-style churches. If you're looking for excellent restaurants and well-populated watering holes, the walking tour can also provide for some very colorful and entertaining afternoons.

For those of you eager to explore areas outside of Nashville via commercial transportation, you will have no problem finding a variety of bus, trolley, and riverboat tours to zip, scoot, or float around town. Nashville also offers a handful of top-notch professional sporting events. World-class art museums, beautiful antebellum plantations, 16 colleges and universities, and numerous cultural attractions all contribute to Nashville's well-deserved nickname: "The Athens of the South."

Nashville is also internationally known for its colorful and educational institutions, ranging from historically-important plantations to culturally-diverse art centers and museums. Fortunately, many of these are clustered fairly close together, allowing you to visit several attractions in a single outing. All reasonably priced, these sites showcase the best of middle Tennessee's cultural, historical, and scientific heritage.

Selected Museums Around the Nashville Area

1	Arts in the Airport, *Nashville*
2	Belle Meade Plantation, *Nashville*
3	Belmont Mansion, *Nashville*
4	Cheekwood, *Nashville*
5	Country Music Hall of Fame & Museum, *Nashville*
6	Cumberland Science Museum, *Nashville*
7	Customs House Museum, *Clarksville*
8	Sam Davis Home, *Smyrna*
9	Discovery Center, *Murfreesboro*
10	Frist Center for the Visual Arts, *Nashville*
11	The Hermitage, *Nashville*
12	Historic Carnton Plantation, *Franklin*
13	Historic Mansker's Station, *Goodlettsville*
14	Nashville Public Library, *Nashville*
15	Oakland's Historic House Museum, *Murfreesboro*
16	The Parthenon, *Nashville*
17	James K. Polk Home, *Columbia*
18	Tennessee Agricultural Museum, *Nashville*
19	Tennessee Historical Commission, *Nashville*
20	Tennessee Historical Society, *Nashville*
21	Tennessee State Museum, *Nashville*
22	Travellers Rest Plantation & Museum, *Nashville*
23	Upper Room Chapel & Museum, *Nashville*
24	Vanderbilt University Fine Arts Gallery, *Nashville*

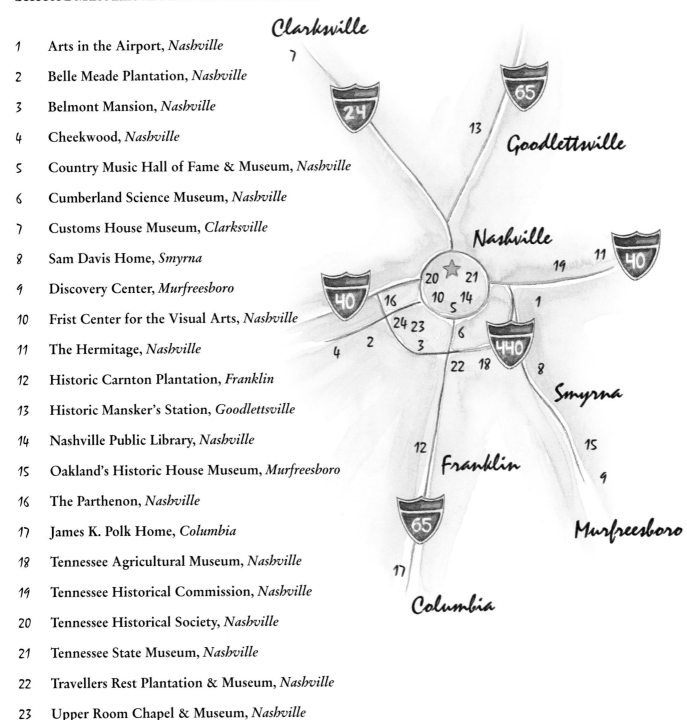

Walking The District
Nashville, Tennessee

Nashville, like every great city, has its *in* place. That place, located alongside the Cumberland River, is referred to as "The District." Walking throughout this area, you will soon discover there are enough attractions to keep you busy for days. Enjoy locations of historical and cultural significance, or simply find a bar stool and spend hours mingling with the crowd. From Irish pubs to dance clubs to blues bars, The District's entertainment choices are endless.

Starting every afternoon and continuing into the early morning hours, The District's honky-tonk locales provide live entertainment to those visiting inside and passing by outside alike. The area is a magnet for those who wish to listen to country music and drink beer. The buildings and warehouses (where many of the lounges are located) might be old, but that doesn't preclude them from hosting some really fantastic entertainment.

If bars and live music fail to hold your interest, you may enjoy a visit to the local music stores that inhabit the strip. Depending on your musical preferences, you can almost certainly find a new, welcome addition to your CD collection.

If interested in musical history, a visit to the nearby Country Music Hall of Fame and Museum or the Ryman Auditorium is strongly recommended. These venues should satisfy anyone's curiosity as to why Nashville enjoys the artistic reputation it does. If you're a sports enthusiast, you will definitely enjoy the nearby Tennessee Sports Hall of Fame, where the state's most memorable sports moments are relived in a state-of-the-art setting. Regardless of your particular interests, a visit to The District is a recipe for a great, rockin' good time!

"Downtown Nashville is so alive. Country music, rock music, whatever music. And people-watching gets no finer than than in The District!"

Kathleen Fleming
Rockabilly Music Connoisseur

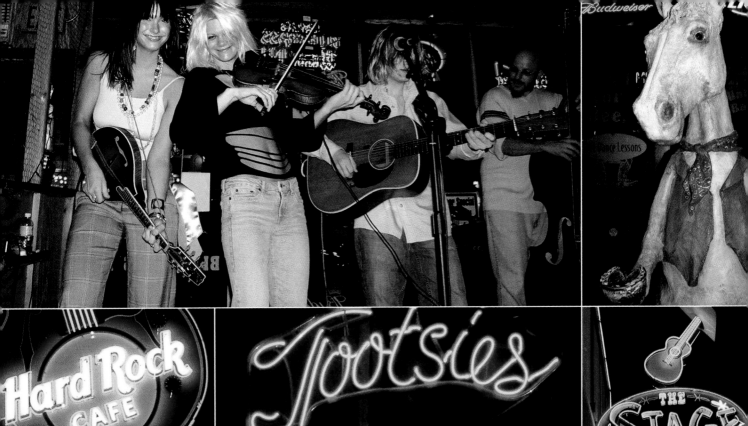

Hard Rock CAFE

Tootsies

THE STAGE ON BROADWAY

RESTAURANT   BIG RIVER   BREWERY

LEGENDS CORNER

PIZZA

FINE FOOD AND BEVERAGES

DELI

★ LIVE ENTERTAINMENT ★

ERNEST TUBB RECORD SHOP

ALL TYPES OF RECORDS SHIPPED AROUND THE WORLD

FREE CATALOG ON REQUEST

REAL COUNTRY MUSIC LIVES HERE EST. 1947

Introduction to Chattanooga
The Reborn City

"One of the top ten overlooked and underrated family destinations."

Fodor's Travel Guide

Older cities sometimes fall into economic and aesthetic decline. This is definitely not the case with Chattanooga. The city's revitalization is the result of a unique public-private partnership, which brought nearly $1.5 billion in development to the downtown area throughout the past two decades. More than $120 million was spent on the riverfront area alone. Chattanooga now has numerous activities for tourists and residents alike, such as the downtown's magnificent Tennessee Aquarium, restaurants, picnic areas, and an interactive water fountain. Downtown Chattanooga, located along a seven-mile bend in the Tennessee River, has a population exceeding 154,000 people and is the hub of attractions and events for the entire family. Free electric shuttle buses give you the opportunity to visit the many locations of of Chattanooga without having to worry about directions or parking. Arts and culture, athletic events, and history all become center stage in one of the most attractive cities of the South.

Chattanooga's beauty, however, extends far beyond the bright lights of the city. A short jaunt past the city limits will lead to thick forests, lush mountains, and peaceful rivers. This spectacular natural beauty provides for breathtaking romantic getaways and enjoyable family vacations. From Lookout Mountain to the many activities on the Tennessee River and Lake Winnepesaukah, you will never be at loss for things to explore in and around one of the South's top tourist destinations.

"Now that the 'new' Chattanooga is being unveiled, one of the top family destinations in the country is even better. We're the best kept secret in the South, and we want to start sharing it with everyone that we can."

Rick Nall
Chattanooga Area
Convention and Visitors Bureau

Lookout Mountain

Chattanooga, Tennessee

It is probably safe to speculate that at some point in his or her lifetime, every Tennessee Valley resident has either visited Chattanooga's Lookout Mountain or at least seen a Lookout Mountain attraction advertised on a barn, billboard, or birdhouse. Rock City, Ruby Falls, and the Incline – none of which is found off the beaten path – are almost as much a part of the Valley's image as the Tennessee River. While school children from around the South periodically visit the mountain, a return trip for adults may well rejuvenate childhood memories and provide a solid day's entertainment for the entire family. You adventuresome folks, however, should not limit yourselves to only visiting the traditional sites. You should explore the entire mountain and seek out its other points of interest. By doing this, you can better appreciate the history of the mountain and all that it represents.

Ruby Falls

Since 1930, millions of visitors have visited the "Jewel of Lookout Mountain," a unique site located hundreds of feet beneath the crest of the mountain. After descending into the mountain by elevator, visitors walk along a cave path to see a new world, filled with geological wonders and numerous rock formations. At the end of the cave path, you'll discover a 145-foot underground waterfall. Named "Ruby Falls" in honor of the wife of one of the original explorers, this waterfall reflects the magnificent beauty of the cavern and is a wondrous and breathtaking sight to behold.

Incline Railway

This railway path has been nicknamed "America's Most Amazing Mile" because the grade of the track reaches 72.7 degrees near the top. This gives the Incline the unique distinction of being the steepest passenger railway in the world! In operation since 1895, the U.S. government designated the railway as both a National Historic Site and a National Historic Mechanical Engineering Landmark. You can depart from either the lower station at the base of Lookout Mountain or the upper station atop the mountain. If the weather cooperates, the stunning view from the observation deck above the upper station allows you to see the Great Smoky Mountains, which are some 100 miles away!

Rock City

This "Citadel of Rocks," first explored in 1823 by two missionaries, was used during the Civil War and later underwent serious development after War War II. Located high atop Lookout Mountain (across Georgia's state line), Rock City has quiet woodland paths and gardens, unique ancient rock formations, and a fairy tale community of sculpted figurines within its walls. One can view seven different states from "Lovers' Leap," experience the "Fat Man's Squeeze," and traverse the "Swing-Along Bridge." Rock City and its gardens are a pleasant treat, especially for those curious about what all of those "See Rock City" barn signs are advertising.

Lookout Mountain – Continued

Point Park

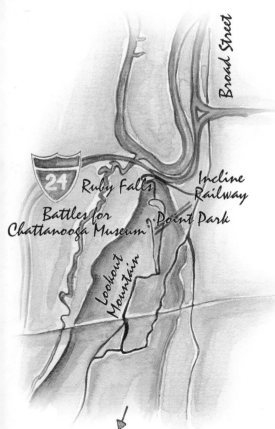

Operated by the National Park Service, Point Park can be found in the Chickamauga and Chattanooga National Military Park. A visitor center, the Ochs Museum, and the Cravens' House (used as headquarters by both Union and Confederate officers) are all located in the park. Within the visitor center is James Walker's dynamic painting entitled "The Battle of Lookout Mountain." Many consider this 30' x 13' painting to be the highlight of the center. Point Park is most often noted as the site of the "Battle Above the Clouds." The true beauty of the park, however, is not found in its historical background, but in its scenic grounds, walking trails, and fantastic overlook of Chattanooga. A visit by the entire family is well worth the trip.

The Battles for Chattanooga Museum

This history buff hot spot is located three blocks from the upper station of the Incline. The museum features a colorful, narrated, three-dimensional electronic map presentation of Chattanooga's major Civil War battles, which took place in November 1863. A booming audio track featuring a rich supply of sound effects contributes greatly to the experience. Using more than 650 lights, the map features 5,000 miniature soldiers and presents a detailed look at the significant engagements that took place around the city. The overview includes the battles of Lookout Mountain, Wauhatchie, Orchard Knob, Brown's Ferry, the charge up Missionary Ridge, and the "Battle Above the Clouds." The museum, which is an excellent starting point for a Civil War tour of the city, includes a relic and weapons collection, as well as a gift shop and bookstore. A solid collection of Civil War books is available for purchase.

The Grand Ole Opry and Grand Ole Opry Museum
Nashville, Tennessee

Few attractions within the Tennessee Valley embody the spirit, history and culture of the region in the way that the Grand Ole Opry does. From Johnny Cash to Dolly Parton, the royalty of country music have been involved in this weekly production since 1925 – just five years after commercial radio was born in the United States. Roy Acuff, Ernest Tubb, Hank Williams, and Patsy Cline are just a few of the musicians who have graced this stage. While many things about the Opry have changed over the years – from its members to its home – the tradition of wonderful music continues. When the big red curtain goes up, visitors know they are in for hours of top-notch entertainment.

The Grand Ole Opry Museum, located adjacent to the Grand Ole Opry House, features everything ranging from instruments to interactive videos to a gift shop. Posters, photographs, guitars and more await visitors to this free facility. The museum is an ideal stop before going to the Opry. Featuring items ranging from one of Minnie Pearl's signature hats to Roy Acuff's fiddles, the museum tells the story of how the Grand Ole Opry became the cornerstone of country music. It pays tribute to the world's longest running radio show and features themed exhibits honoring the greatest stars of the Grand Ole Opry.

Fall Creek Falls
Pikeville, Tennessee

Fall Creek Falls State Resort Park serves as home to some of middle Tennessee's most breathtaking natural rock formations. It is Tennessee's largest state park, with more than 22,000 acres. In addition to a stunning 256-foot waterfall (after which the park is named), the area features a variety of other beautiful falls, cascades, gorges and streams that kids, adults, and even the family dog can all enjoy. Hiking and biking paths weave their way through the hickory and oak forests that cover the park. Some trails are more difficult than others – visitors should consult trail maps before venturing out. Visitors to Fall Creek Falls can also enjoy fishing and boating on its 345-acre lake. Privately-owned boats are not allowed – however, canoes, aluminum fishing boats and pedal boats are all available for rent through the park office. State records for both bluegill and channel catfish have been set on the lake. With picnic facilities, cabins, a restaurant, campgrounds, and special events ranging from rock climbing workshops to backpacking excursions, this weekend getaway is a must for Tennessee Valley residents.

FALL CREEK FALLS ⇨

"With its breathtaking waterfalls, stunning canyons, and lush forests, Fall Creek Falls State Park has enough beauty to refresh even the weariest of travelers. And with its well thought-out facilities, and numerous nature programs, it becomes a natural destination for families and others seeking to get away."

Stuart Carroll
Interpretive Specialist
Fall Creek Falls State Park

The University of the South

Sewanee, Tennessee

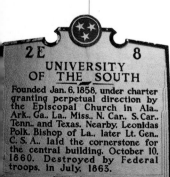

Officials at almost every college or university are generally quick to brag about the beauty and architectural splendor of their campuses. Before those individuals get too carried away with self-serving compliments, it is recommended they visit Franklin County's University of the South (popularly known as Sewanee). Located atop the Cumberland Plateau, this university is one of America's most distinctive college campuses. With the exception of the magnificent All Saints Chapel, the major facilities were constructed between 1875 and 1915 and built of local Sewanee sandstone. The buildings have a Gothic-style architecture, similar to those found on the campuses of Oxford or Cambridge. Regardless of collegiate loyalty or religious preference, a visit to Sewanee with a leisurely stroll through the grounds provides a truly enjoyable outing.

Coolidge Park
Chattanooga, Tennessee

Once an abandoned shipping yard, Coolidge Park has carried the spirit of revitalization from downtown to the North Shore. Located on Chattanooga's River Street, the park is a fantastic place to take the kids on a family trip. Named in honor of Charles Coolidge, a World War II Medal of Honor recipient, the area is part of the Tennessee Riverpark, a continuous range of parks, trails, and landmarks along the Tennessee River. You can play in an interactive fountain, stroll on the Walnut Street Bridge (the world's longest pedestrian bridge), enjoy a picnic along the river's shore, or ride the three-row, vintage carousel. The carousel, built in 1895, is fitted with 52 beautifully-carved animal seats. On a sunny afternoon, you will find people throwing Frisbees, flying kites, or just lounging around enjoying the beautiful scenery. The park itself is located adjacent to numerous unique shops, galleries, and restaurants, which make this recreational area a wonderful afternoon destination for young and old alike.

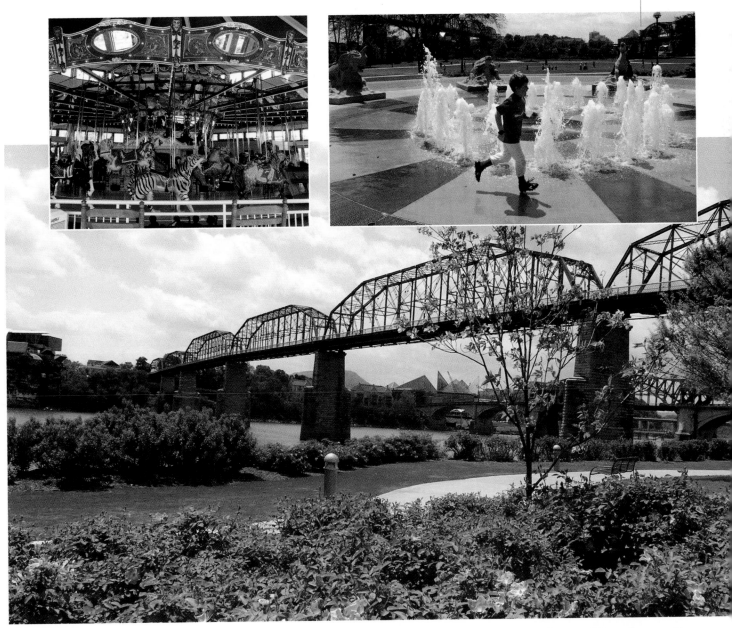

Jack Daniel Distillery
Lynchburg, Tennessee

Listed in the National Register of Historic Places, the Jack Daniel Distillery is the nation's oldest registered distillery. Located in historic Lynchburg, Tennessee, the distillery features a large, modern, and attractive visitor center exhibit hall. The center also displays a short movie discussing the distillery's founder, Jack Daniel, and the sour mash whiskey making process he perfected in 1866. Following a stroll through the visitor center, you whiskey lovers can take a one-hour guided bus tour of the distillery. Once inside the building, enjoy a walk-through of the facilities, where you'll learn the science behind Jack Daniel's whiskey production. While there, be sure to sample the sour mash in the distillery, as well as purchase a commemorative decanter of whiskey – which is legally available for sale in this otherwise dry county.

Tennessee Sports Hall of Fame
Nashville, Tennessee

Located in the Gaylord Entertainment Center, this museum is a state-of-the-art 7,200-square-foot interactive facility that recounts the best moments in Tennessee's rich sports history. It traces a variety of sports dating back to the 1800s. The museum provides interactive entertainment in the way of virtual competition against computerized players in different sports. It also features special exhibits on Tennessee Olympians and showcases numerous scenes from a variety of sporting events. From kayaking on the Ocoee River to breathtaking moments of the college gridiron, the Hall offers sporting displays from both past and present that are sure to please even the biggest of couch potatoes.

"Go one-on-one with a former Lady Vol All-American in the Tennessee Sports Hall of Fame Museum. Learn about former Olympic stars like Wilma Rudolph then visit our college football area where you'll see all the greats ... from 1886 to the present. Tennessee Titans, Nashville Predators, minor league baseball, ... you'll enjoy all this and more."

Ryland Hoskins
Director
Tennessee Sports Hall of Fame

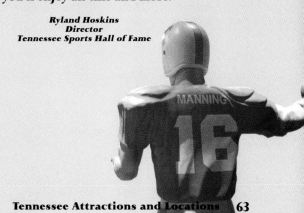

The Parthenon
Nashville, Tennessee

Located in beautiful Centennial Park, the Parthenon is more than just a building or museum – it is a well-documented history lesson. The city of Nashville first undertook the construction of this full-scale Parthenon replica to house the international art section of the 1897 Centennial Exposition. By 1921, the building was in such poor condition that the Park Board authorized its reconstruction, both inside and out. On May 21, 1931, the city reopened the Parthenon to the public with a vast array of galleries and exhibits. The

majority of the collections, many of which are rotated out approximately every six weeks, are found on the lower level of the building. The area also displays numerous television consoles discussing the building, its history, and some of the various exhibits on display. The upper level houses one of Nashville's most famous structures, the majestic statue of Athena. Standing almost 42 feet tall, it is the largest piece of indoor sculpture in the western world. According to Greek mythology, Athena (the goddess of wisdom, prudent warfare, and the arts) was born from the head of Zeus, chief of all the gods. The upper floor also features the *Naos*, *Elgin Casts*, *Treasury*, and the *Pediment* models.

Tennessee River Museum
Savannah, Tennessee

Have you ever wondered why the cities that make up the Tennessee Valley developed where they did? The Tennessee River's historic influence on the people and culture of this region has been significant, to say the least. Located near Shiloh National Military Park and Pickwick Landing State Park, this small, attractive museum is a monument to the river and the impact it has made throughout the centuries. In addition to exhibits involving the area's paleontology and archaeology, the museum also details the military and commercial history of the Tennessee River. These exhibits include informative displays on the early steamboats that traversed the waters of the area. You will enter the *War on the River* exhibit room through a half-scale model of the bow of the ill-fated gunboat U.S.S. Cairo. Upon entering this exhibit, you will learn about the critical role the river played in the Union Army's invasion routes. In the *Army* exhibit, glass display cases present examples of personal items, munitions, and weaponry typical of Civil War-era foot soldiers. In total, the Tennessee River Museum features five major exhibits, as well as a gift shop. The museum also presents an interesting collection of field artillery shells. Numerous old photos from the surrounding areas accompany the Civil War-era artifacts. This museum is an educational primer for anyone planning to visit the nearby Shiloh National Military Park, and qualifies as a particularly enjoyable treat for history buffs.

"This private museum represents a tribute to the Tennessee River and its influence on the land, people and heritage of the Tennessee Valley. From dinosaurs to the TVA, anyone interested in learning about the lower Tennessee River valley region will find the area's history unique and fascinating."

Jim Parris
Curator
Tennessee River Museum

The Tennessee Antebellum Trail

Weekend adventurers often overlook published, planned driving excursions. The Tennessee Antebellum Trail offers an entertaining, scenic, and educational driving opportunity allowing you to visit homes, plantations, and historic markers at your leisure. Although some selected homes from the Antebellum Trail are featured elsewhere in this publication, the trail described below enables you to see some of the grandest homes found within the state. In addition to the seven designated homes, you will discover more than 50 roadside markers along your journey. These markers are adorned with the Antebellum Trail symbol identifying other historic sites in middle Tennessee. This 90-mile loop, which starts south of Nashville, identifies the following homes that are open to the public:

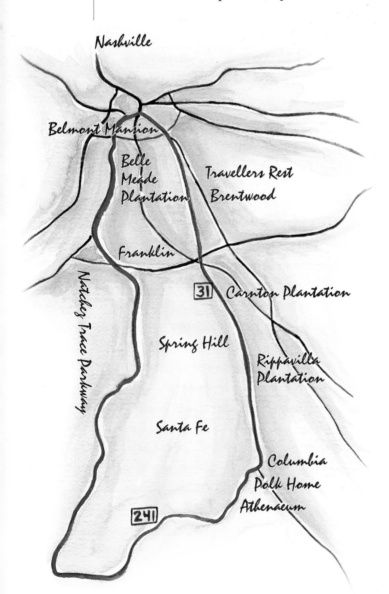

Belmont Mansion – Completed in 1853, this grand estate consists of a beautiful 36-room mansion and surrounding grounds. With furnishings and art works, it is the largest historic house museum in Tennessee.

Belle Meade Plantation – "The Queen of Tennessee Plantations" is the scene of a skirmish that took place during the Battle of Nashville. The plantation later developed a worldwide reputation as a top thoroughbred horse farm and first-class breeding establishment. The 30-acre site contains eight historic buildings, including a stable that houses an antique carriage collection. Costumed guides conduct regular tours.

Travellers Rest Plantation – This plantation served as the Confederacy's headquarters prior to the Battle of Nashville. It contains an interactive museum that interprets the city's historic past. It is Nashville's oldest historic home still open to the public.

Carnton Plantation – This beautifully restored neoclassical plantation home was used as a Confederate field hospital during the Battle of Franklin. Adjacent to the plantation is the largest private Confederate cemetery in the country.

Rippavilla Plantation – Built in 1852, this 12,000-square-foot plantation home contains a museum dedicated to the Civil War armies of Tennessee. It also serves as a regional visitor center.

James K. Polk Home – A Federal-style residence built in 1816, by James Polk's father, this became home to our country's 11th president. The museum displays original belongings, as well as White House artifacts and memorabilia of both President and Mrs. Polk.

Athenaeum Rectory – Built in 1835 by President Polk's nephew, this home served as the official rectory to The Athenaeum, a prestigious girls school located in downtown Columbia. The Rectory now contains a public tearoom and house museum.

A one to two-day drive along this trail reveals a colorful, informative look at local history. Even if you choose to visit only a few of the homes and sites listed, the trail provides an experience not easily forgotten. Prior to starting out, it is recommended you pick up an Antebellum Trail guide.

*"Every site along the Antebellum Trail was touched by the war as both Union
and Confederate forces commandeered housing and provisions."*

The Tennessee Antebellum Trail Guide

Nashville Zoo
Nashville, Tennessee

Lemurs and tigers and birds, oh my! Indeed, the Nashville Zoo at Grassmere is one of the Valley's best places to go critter-watching. From majestic Bengal tigers and splendidly colored macaws, to creepy-looking arachnids, giant lumbering elephants, and menacing alligators, you can get your fill of extraordinary life forms here. For a very reasonable entry fee, the zoo features animal shows, aquariums, an amphitheater, and informative displays to help you understand more about the natural world. This is, understandably, an especially popular and educational attraction for visitors of all ages.

"The zoo is so much fun. Some of the animals don't even seem real because they are so weird looking."

Jorrell Domingo
World's Biggest Lizard Fan

Creative Discovery Museum
Chattanooga, Tennessee

Located two blocks from the Tennessee Aquarium and the IMAX 3D Theater, the Creative Discovery Museum is a fantastic place to take little ones in need of entertainment. Designed especially for children ages 12 and under, this museum is packed full of hands-on family activities. The facilities have a host of friendly staff members to answer questions and assist children in their various activities. And children have plenty of entertainment options to choose from. In the *Musician's Studio*, children can create their own music, and in the *Excavation Station*, they can search for lost dinosaur bones. Aspiring inventors can visit the *Inventor's Clubhouse*, where they can build robots and perform various science experiments. The *RiverPlay* exhibit teaches youngsters about rivers, locks, and dams. For the athletic types, the Creative Discovery Museum features a multitude of pulleys and climbing structures on the *Rooftop Fun Factory.* This area is particularly helpful in allowing the sparkplugs of the group to expend their energies! The museum also has a café and a gift shop available during regular operating hours.

Southern Belle
Chattanooga, Tennessee

Experienced travelers visiting a city for the first time often take bus tours to familiarize themselves with the city's history and major features. In Chattanooga, one enjoyable alternative to this practice is to take a trip on the Southern Belle, which is docked at Ross's Landing. This 500-passenger climate-controlled riverboat provides an enjoyable and relaxing way to explore the area. The captain narrates a running commentary on the city and features of the surrounding countryside. Floating down the Tennessee River while learning about the city of Chattanooga provides a fantastic way to spend a lazy afternoon. And it all comes with a nice view of the ever-impressive Lookout Mountain.

"A boat ride on the Southern Belle is a real nice way

to see and learn about Chattanooga."

John Bedingfield
Boaz, Alabama

The Home of Buford Pusser
Adamsville, Tennessee

A visit to the Sheriff Buford Pusser Home and Museum provides a look into the residence, furnishings, and memorabilia of the South's most legendary lawman. The subject of three *Walking Tall* films and a TV documentary entitled *The Great American Hero*, Buford Pusser was the target of numerous assassination attempts – one of which resulted in the death of his wife. The museum has many exhibits that document the man and his career. Pusser was shot eight times, knifed seven times, and once fought off six men during a brawl. Adamsville hosts an annual three-day Sheriff Buford Pusser Festival, featuring a variety of family activities in honor of this American hero.

Downtown Lynchburg
Lynchburg, Tennessee

Just as Chattanooga and Nashville have downtowns that deserve spotlighting, so does the Tennessee city of Lynchburg. Downtown Lynchburg, however, is noteworthy for all of the reasons the other cities are not. This town's center is a very small, very eclectic, very Southern collection of antique shops and curiosities. You will likely spot numerous motorcyclists traveling to and from the city, as the roads leading into and out of Lynchburg are among the most scenic in the Valley. Not surprisingly, the nearby distillery has influenced downtown Lynchburg, with Jack Daniel references and memorabilia peppering the scenery. The town square is a rather picturesque addition to the area, one which deserves a stop and a stroll if you choose to visit any nearby areas or attractions.

Cumberland Trail
Southeast Tennessee

The Cumberland Trail is pure Tennessee. It presents breathtaking scenery and invigorating hiking trails. Best of all, this scenic area is not plagued with a high number of visitors. Instead, it provides for a simple, quiet, fantastic getaway. Located west of the Tennessee River along the rugged eastern escarpment of the Cumberland Plateau, the 300-plus miles of planned footpaths begin in Kentucky's Cumberland Gap National Park. The main trail then stretches south to Signal Point National Historic Park and to the Prentice Cooper Wildlife Management Area located just outside Chattanooga. The Tennessee section of the trail is being built and maintained in a cooperative effort between the Cumberland Trail Conference (CTC), private partners (such as Bowater Corporation), and the state of Tennessee. The CTC and its hundreds of volunteers are leading efforts in the construction and maintenance of the Cumberland Trail. Once completed, the trail will pass through a total of 11 Tennessee counties. More than 168 miles are currently open to the public, and more miles are opening on a monthly basis. A number of sections near paved trailheads are designed for inexperienced hikers and those with disabilities. Other sections are a bit more challenging. Along the trail, you will encounter spectacular remote overlooks, narrow footbridges, beautiful waterfalls, and clear, deep-running streams. Unlike the famous driveable Natchez Trace which runs between Nashville and Natchez, Mississippi, the Cumberland Trail is too rugged for motorized vehicles of any kind. This is a trail being built by hikers for hikers – and volunteers are always encouraged to come and work on trails and bridges. Of course, if you are interested simply in hiking, backpacking, or kayaking, you will find this trail makes for a wonderful weekend destination.

Cumberland Gap

Cove Lake State Park   LaFollette
Frozen Head State Park   Caryville

Cumberland Mountain   Wartburg
State Park (Crossville)
                        Crab Orchard

                        Spring City

North Chickamauga   Dayton
Creek Gorge SNA

                    Soddy-Daisy

Prentice Cooper SF   Chattanooga

"The Cumberland State Scenic Trail is Tennessee's first linear state park. Its completion will take the hiker along more than 300 miles of natural splendor, from Chattanooga on its southern end to the Cumberland Gap at the Tennessee-Kentucky-Virginia line. Along the way, the Cumberland Trail crosses at least two routes of the Trail of Tears, and courses along bluffs, creek gorges, and diverse flora and fauna that are the signature of the Cumberland Plateau."

Paul Freeman
Executive Director
Cumberland Trail Conference

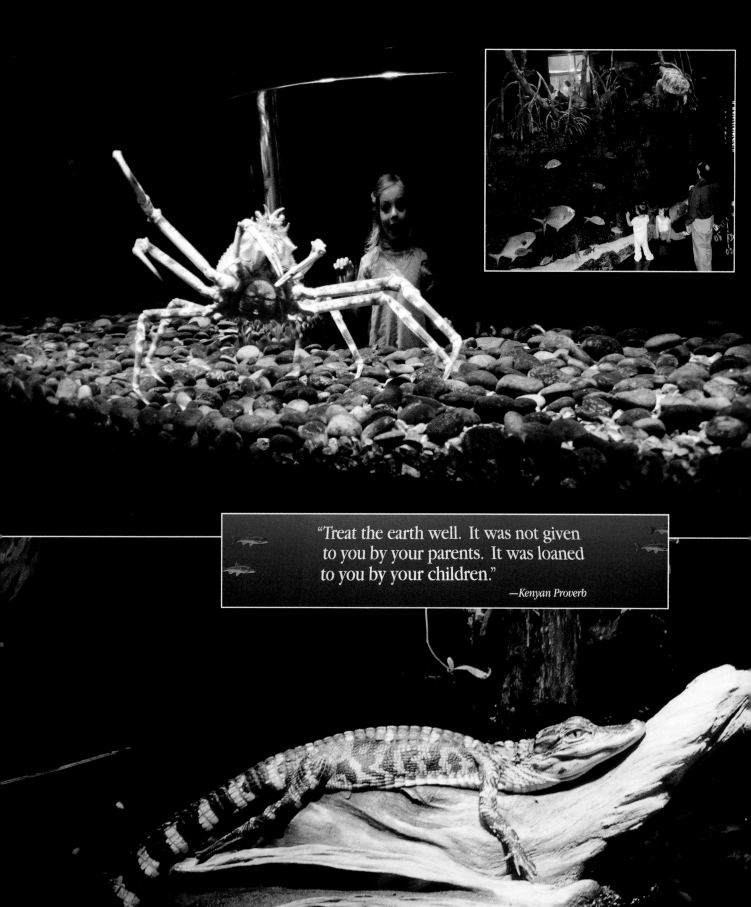

"Treat the earth well. It was not given to you by your parents. It was loaned to you by your children."

—*Kenyan Proverb*

Tennessee Aquarium
Chattanooga, Tennessee

Of all the tourist locations in the Tennessee Valley, the Tennessee Aquarium may very well rank as the most popular destination of them all. Since opening in 1992, the aquarium has attracted more than a million customers per year. Its freshwater facility, one of the world's largest, is named *River Journey*, and contains approximately 400,000 gallons of water. It traces the Tennessee River as it winds from the Smoky Mountains into the Ohio River, flows into the Mississippi River, and then eventually empties down into the Gulf of Mexico. Inside the towering, peaked buildings reside a multitude of exhibits and displays – from trout and whimsical sea dragons to fascinating environmental exhibits that entertain both children and adults. In addition to the indoor facilities, visitors can step outside to view beautiful gardens and waterfalls. These help depict the natural habitats of some 9,000 swimming, crawling, and flying creatures. Supplementing *River Journey* is the newer, modernistic *Ocean Journey*, a 700,000-gallon seawater addition to the freshwater exhibit hall. In this aquarium, you can get an eye-to-eye view of squid, crabs, sharks, stingrays, and numerous other sea creatures. Nearby, the Tennessee Aquarium's IMAX 3D Theater will wow you with a six-story screen, digital surround sound, and cutting-edge technology. This facility educates and entertains in a way that standard movie theaters simply cannot. Whether it be the freshwater aquarium, the saltwater aquarium, or the IMAX theater that piques your interest, a tour of the Tennessee Aquarium is a must for all Valley-area visitors.

"The Museum's goal is to engage visitors in the breadth and minutiae of the country music story in the context of local and national history."

John Rumble
Senior Historian
Country Music Hall of Fame
and Museum

Country Music Hall of Fame and Museum

Nashville, Tennessee

A tour of this modern, $37 million, 130,000-square-foot museum offers a first-hand look at how country music has evolved throughout the years. The museum exhibits are organized chronologically starting with the early roots of country music. Listening booths are set up so you can better appreciate the different tunes of each country music era. See vintage automobiles, rare costumes, films, live performances, and interactive exhibits. The facilities feature a computer-archive arcade, a beautiful Hall of Fame rotunda, four theaters, and numerous rooms and galleries holding thousands of items of memorabilia. Museum historians and curators are also available to answer your questions. You can even create customized CDs at the burning stations located outside the Star Experience Theater. Regardless of whether you are a serious country music fan, casual listener, or curious passerby in search of something interesting, this is an enjoyable, crowd-pleasing place to visit.

Cumberlands Craft Trail
Middle Tennessee

The Cumberlands Craft Trail is a geographical area in middle Tennessee extending south from Lebanon to Tullahoma. Within this region lie approximately 45 identified commercial stores and cottage industries producing, among other items, glassware, pottery, baskets, jewelry, wood carvings, sculptures, and paintings. Some of the establishments are so particular about the products they carry that they use a panel of craftsmen to help them decide. Trail routes lead you through rolling hills and down back roads, while providing scenic views that allow you to appreciate middle Tennessee's less-populated areas. The trail features the works of both small-time cottage industries and large-scale craft companies. Five partnering organizations sponsor the craft trail, several of which are nonprofit educational entities. The primary goal of these organizations is the preservation of artistic traditions and the enhancement of quality craftsmanship. The Cumberlands Craft Trail is a nice opportunity to get away from the mainstream of the city while viewing some beautiful Tennessee countryside along the way.

Traveling Glory Land Road
Southeastern Tennessee

The Valley's music, food, dress, and literature are all heavily derived from its residents' religious and spiritual beliefs. Anyone interested in learning about the area's religious history should consider spending some time traveling on the "Glory Land Road." The result of a two-year project by the Southeast Tennessee Tourism Association, Glory Land Road is a self-guided driving tour. The route includes 16 major sites, identified and discussed in a published brochure available at www.southeast-tennessee.com. Beginning in downtown Chattanooga and winding through individual counties into the "Great Valley," the brochure details everything from the region's many religious museums and faith-based colleges to "Decoration Day," a time-honored annual family tradition largely unheard of outside the Deep South. The brochure contains a religious timeline and details the events, individuals, and back-country churches that significantly impacted the religions of the area. With highlights ranging from the attempted Christian conversion of the Cherokee to the Scopes Monkey Trial to the Pentecostal revival, this journey provides insight into the area's diverse religious history. Although this trail is only partially located in the area of the Tennessee Valley discussed by *52 Weekends*, anyone who spends time on the trail will get a better appreciation of the rich religious heritage integral to the Valley's history.

"The trail blows apart the stereotypes, once you see the diversity of beliefs that flourished in this area."

Linda Caldwell
Director
Tennessee Overhill Heritage Association

Bluff View Art District
Chattanooga, Tennessee

Adjacent to both the Hunter and Houston museums and located downtown on the bluffs overlooking the Tennessee River, the Bluff View Art District provides a wide array of artistic and cultural entertainment. Travel to the District to view the art galleries, dine in the unique restaurants, or shop in its many quaint stores. You can even play boccie ball at the Boccie Court Terrace. Everyone should visit the River Gallery Sculpture Garden, which features a permanent collection as well as seasonal exhibits. This garden provides both a relaxing walk and an enjoyable, scenic river view. When visiting all the buildings within the District, you should obtain the free self-guided walking tour pamphlet. The brochure describes the historical buildings as well as the many structures and gardens located within this attractive area.

"Bluff View Art District represents a creative haven for visual and culinary arts."

Jennifer McCormick
Marketing and Sales Director
Bluff View Art District

* Russell Whiting, *Icarus,* located in the Bluff View Art District
** Don Haugen & Teena Stern, *On The Edge,* located in the Bluff View Art District

The Travels of Tennessee's Davy Crockett
Throughout Middle Tennessee

When people hear references to Tennessee's very own Davy Crockett, a wide variety of images often spring to mind. Some envision the made-for-TV Hollywood version while others think of a politician whose charm and humor gained many admirers throughout the country. Some immediately associate Davy Crockett with the courageous defenders of the Alamo, fighting for Texas sovereignty. Above all, most people know Crockett's reputation as a superb backwoods hunter and outdoorsman.

Crockett, who preferred to be called David, was a rugged outdoorsman who often wore buckskins and a coonskin cap. Born in Green County in 1786, he and his wife Polly moved to Lincoln County in 1811, where they settled on the Mulberry Fork of the Elk River. In 1813, he moved to Franklin County, Tennessee. After Polly died in 1815, he met and married Elizabeth Patton and moved to what became Lawrence County, Tennessee. In 1822, he moved to Obion River where he served first in the state legislature and later in the U.S. House of Representatives. Due partially to his stand against the Indian Removal Bill, he was defeated and removed from office in 1831. In 1836, he went to Texas to fight against Mexico for Texas's freedom. Crockett was killed by Mexican General Santa Anna's army on March 6, 1836.

Battlefield Homes of Franklin

Franklin, Tennessee

While there are many Civil War homes and plantations throughout the Valley open to the public, Franklin, Tennessee features two homes especially popular with history buffs. The Carter House and the Carnton Plantation were at the forefront of the Battle of Franklin. The Carter House, built in 1830, was caught in the center of the battle, and the Carter family and friends hid in the cellar during the gruesome five-hour exchange. Today, the facility features a video presentation, a museum, and a guided tour of the house and grounds. Located a short driving distance away is the Carnton Plantation. On the afternoon of November 30, 1864, the home became a Confederate field hospital for hundreds of troops. When the house eventually overflowed with the injured and dying, soldiers were put in the yards surrounding the house. In 1978, a private foundation, the Carnton Association, obtained the property and slowly restored it to the beautiful antebellum mansion that now welcomes visitors throughout the year. Within walking distance of the Carnton Plantation is the attractive and well-maintained McGavock Confederate Cemetery. A resting place for some 1,500 CSA soldiers, it is the largest private Confederate cemetery in the country.

3D 34 CARTER HOUSE

Built 1830 by Fountain Branch Carter, and in use by three generations of his family. Here was command post of Maj. Gen. Jacob D. Cox, Federal field commander of Schofield's delaying action. The hottest fighting took place just east and south nearby. Capt. Theodoric Carter, C SA, a son of the family, was mortally wounded.

TENNESSEE HISTORICAL COMMISSION

CARNTON PLANTATION

Carnton was built ca. 1815 by Randal McGavock (1768-1843), planter, political leader and mayor of Nashville. Named after the McGavock home in Northern Ireland, the house was greatly enlarged by Randal ca. 1826. His son, John, later added the Greek Revival porches, one of which served as an observation post for Gen. Nathan B. Forrest during the Battle of Franklin, Nov. 30, 1864. After the Battle, Carnton served as a hospital. The bodies of Generals Adams, Cleburne, Granbury, and Strahl rested on the back porch the next morning. Carnton was acquired by the Carnton Association in 1978.

WILLIAMSON COUNTY HISTORICAL SOCIETY, 1994

Old Stone Fort State Park
Manchester, Tennessee

In the city of Manchester, Tennessee, you can find one of the most interesting state parks in the Valley area. At first, you might assume from the park's name that it is some type of historical military fortification. In actuality, it is a 2,000-year-old American Indian ceremonial site. The "fort" itself is nestled within the forks of a river and is basically

a wall enclosure composed of humus, clay, and rock. Not surprisingly, this wall has somewhat blended throughout the centuries into its surroundings and at first glance might appear to be a peculiar natural hill formation. The walking trail along the mounds provides beautiful views, most notably of the cliffs above the rivers and the various waterfalls. You are encouraged to stop in and visit the park museum, which houses a selection of ancient Native American artifacts and informative audio-visual presentations.

Natchez Trace Parkway
From Nashville to Natchez

Extending south from Nashville through northwestern Alabama and into Mississippi, the 444-mile Natchez Trace Parkway provides a wonderful weekend getaway for families who wish to enjoy a scenic drive through beautiful countryside. The Trace, which was started as a Native American trail by Natchez, Chickasaw, and Choctaw Indians, later became a popular trading route between Nashville and Natchez for woodsmen. Operated by the National Park Service, the Parkway parallels the Old Trace and provides a history lesson for those eager to learn more about this famous byway. Learn about the

many early explorers and military men, including General Andrew Jackson, who used the trail for quick passage through this area. At milepost 386, you will come across the 300-acre site of the Meriwether Lewis Monument. This historic marker identifies the location of where this famous explorer mysteriously died (or was murdered, depending upon which book you read) in 1809. Numerous other historic markers are located along the Trace, providing a wealth of information certain to educate and entertain. At the northern end of the Parkway, there are 24 miles of trails within the Leipers Fork District near Franklin, which are popular for hiking, biking, and horseback riding. The Tennessee Valley section of the Natchez Trace provides and preserves an important example of our nation's natural and cultural heritage.

Ryman Auditorium
Nashville, Tennessee

Designated as a National Historic Landmark in 2001 and identified by Travelocity as one of the "10 Coolest Values" in the world, the Ryman Auditorium stands as an icon to country music. As the former home of the Grand Ole Opry (1943-1974), the Ryman is a tradition in itself. It was built in 1892 by Captain Thomas Ryman, a steamboat captain and prominent Nashville businessman. For decades, many of the world's greatest stars performed in front of adoring fans in this building. Renovated in 1993, the auditorium now has a performance hall which eloquently reflects the music played by its many diverse groups. There is also a self-guided tour available which takes you through the "Mother Church of Country Music" on a 100-year voyage throughout music history. It is now a state-of-the-art facility that pays weekly tribute to both the most popular modern-day music entertainers as well as the best country musicians of years past. If you aren't able to visit the auditorium in the evening to catch any of the live performances, a daytime tour is available.

*Tennessee sculptor Russ Faxon, *Oh Roy*, bronze sculpture of Roy Acuff and Minnie Pearl, Courtesy of Ryman Auditorium

Amish Country
Ethridge, Tennessee

"The Amish live this way not because they have any religious convictions against these innovations themselves, but because they believe their unique way of life – which emphasizes humility, simplicity, sharing, and sacrifice – cannot be lived with the distractions of modern life."

Robert Brandt
Touring the
Middle Tennessee Backroads

The Amish, also known as "The Gentle People" or "The Plain Folk," settled in Lawrence County in 1944. Named after their founder, Jacob Amman, who first started the group in Europe around 1695, they migrated from Ohio and then later from Indiana in the late 1940s. There are approximately 200 families in the Ethridge area. The Amish follow a strict set of rules – they live without telephones, electricity, or automobiles. The pace of life in this area, located north of Lawrenceburg, is a bit less frantic than what many of us are accustomed to. Horse-drawn black buggies traverse the countryside. The Amish believe their way of life, which emphasizes humility and simplicity, is preferable to the modern ways most of us enjoy. Amish families keep their children out of public schools and many often speak German. The Amish have a reputation for being highly efficient farmers and expert craftspeople. Some of their most popular commercial articles are available for purchase at local craft stores, including hickory-bent rocking chairs, quilts, swings, and baskets. Although you can purchase some of these items at their homes, it is important to respect their privacy. Visiting the Amish in Ethridge can certainly be an eye-opening, cultural experience.

Adventure Science Center
Nashville, Tennessee

Nashville's Adventure Science Center is a private, non-profit educational institution. Its mission is to inspire children, parents, and teachers by facilitating the learning of science in a dynamic, interactive environment. Above all else, it strives to be fun! The Center features numerous hands-on exhibits that challenge participants in a wide variety of activities. From testing physical strength and coordination to discovering fascinating curiosities about the human body, this high-energy museum manages to teach and entertain all at once. In the center of the building is a 75-foot *Adventure Tower*, which contains educational activities representing the museum's six scientific concept areas: *Earth Science, Creativity & Invention, Sound & Light, Air & Space, Health,* and *Energy*. The Center also contains a

full-motion flight simulator, fossil digs, a World Theater, a planetarium, and much more. Presentations from outside organizations (such as NASA and the Banard-Seyfert Astronomical Society) often enhance visitors' experiences. The Adventure Science Center is similar to a big, fun-filled, thought-provoking science class – but without all the pesky homework!

"We are proud to consistently provide hands-on, engaging exhibits that foster growth and encourage imagination and curiosity."

Ralph Schulz
CEO
Adventure Science Center

Chattanooga Market
Chattanooga, Tennessee

The Chattanooga Market, also known as "Sunday on the Southside," offers something for everyone. Open every Sunday from mid-April through December, the market features numerous booths brimming with handcrafted items, demonstrations, homemade goodies, artifacts, and various artworks produced by regional artisans. Fresh produce and a wide variety of foods are also available to sample and purchase. Every Sunday, a number of colorful events take place on the stage, including live music from a wide variety of musical groups. If you tire of wandering from booth to booth, you can always stop in and grab lunch at the Market Café. The Chattanooga Market publishes an event schedule every Spring detailing the entertainment and events that will be provided throughout the year.

Falls Mill

Belvidere, Tennessee

On the banks of Factory Creek in Belvidere, Tennessee, lies beautiful Falls Mill. This unique establishment provides you with a snapshot of industrial and agricultural history. Falls Mill is an old-fashioned operating water-powered grain mill. This attraction holds great appeal for those interested in the antique machinery and processes used in both the printing of early documents and the grinding of agricultural products. Built in 1873 as a cotton and woolen factory, the mill was later converted – first for use as a cotton gin and then as a woodworking shop. Today, a 32-foot water wheel powers millstones that grind cornmeal, flour, and grits. The building containing the mill also houses a two-story museum where you can see a printing press, hand looms, power looms, spinning wheels, and wool-carding machinery. Falls Mill even has a dog-powered butter churn. Products from the mill, such as cornmeal, grits, and flour can all be purchased on site. Adjacent to the mill is a bed and breakfast log cabin for overnight guests.

1915 WITTE
one-cylinder gasoline engine
6-horsepower
Used in Arkansas to drive
small feed grinding mill.
still operable.

Tennessee State Museum
Nashville, Tennessee

Anyone interested in learning not only about Tennessee, but also about the South in general, should visit this state-run museum. One of the most impressive features of the Tennessee State Museum is the size of the facility. It is one of the largest state museums in the country, featuring more than 60,000 square feet of permanent exhibits and a 10,000-square-foot temporary exhibition hall. Located within walking distance from downtown Nashville, the museum's interpretive exhibits begin 15,000 years ago and continue through to the early 1900s. All major aspects of Tennessee's history are explored in this enjoyable and well-designed environment. The prehistoric, frontier, age of Jackson, antebellum, Civil War, and Reconstruction periods are each represented. The museum also displays many types of unusual items and furniture representing each era. Famous citizens of the state – such as Andrew Jackson, David Crockett, Sam Houston, Alvin York, and Cordell Hull – come alive through interesting displays and one-of-a-kind memorabilia. Peruse displays detailing the women's suffrage movement, or explore art and cultural exhibitions throughout the facility. The Military Museum (a branch of the Tennessee State Museum located across the street from the main facility) covers overseas conflicts beginning with the Spanish-American War and progressing through to the events of World War II.

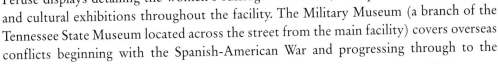

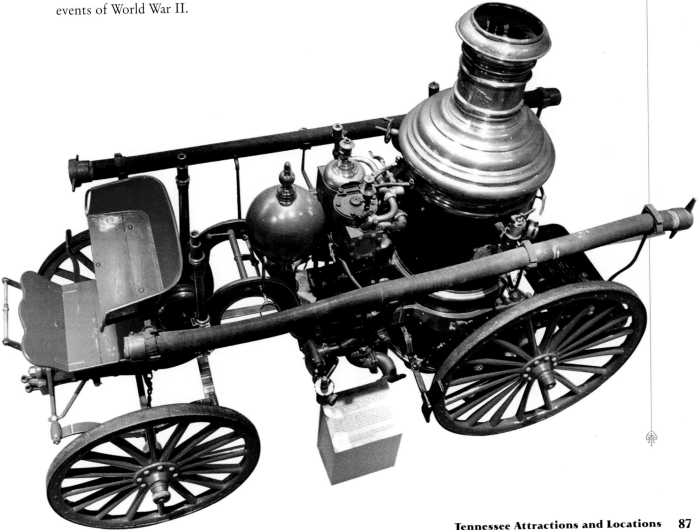

Chattanooga
African-American Museum
Chattanooga, Tennessee

This museum, established in 1983, is dedicated to discovering and preserving achievements of African-Americans, particularly those who have lived in Chattanooga. You'll first view the *Wall of Respect*, which honors Chattanooga's African-Americans for their impressive accomplishments as leaders in their respective fields. The museum's other sections include *Families and Neighborhoods*, *Arts and Entertainment*, *Sports*, *Civil Rights and Politics*, *Churches and Religion*, *Military and Wars*, and *Business and Industry*. The wide array of displays range from Ethiopian church re-creations to descriptions of 12th century African cities. Other attractions include selected artifacts from the life of Bessie Smith (the "Empress of the Blues"), and historical overviews of early African-Americans in Chattanooga. All subjects and displays are enhanced through the rich use of photographs, documents, and three-dimensional artifacts. The museum also houses a research library and a gift shop featuring a variety of African and African-American materials. This is one of the Tennessee Valley's more important cultural centers, offering a unique history lesson that should not be missed.

"History has been made,

it is up to us to preserve it."

Vilma Scruggs Fields
Executive Director
Chattanooga African-American Museum

Hang Gliding at Flight Park
Chattanooga / Trenton, Georgia

"It was scary at first, especially when the tow rope released. Then it became exciting and fun."

Mason Stanford
Knoxville, Tennessee
Age 12

The Tennessee Valley is noted for many activities, ranging from musical festivals to tractor pulls. One feature unique to the Tennessee Valley is the country's largest hang gliding school. Lookout Mountain Flight Park, a 44-acre mountain resort with lodging accommodations for its students, conducts a multitude of training packages for novices and experts alike. From introductory tandem flights to advanced solo flights off the top of the mountain, this school has something for thrill seekers of all ages. Flight Park houses a variety of aircraft, including hang gliders, ultralights, and "trikes" (motorized hang gliders). With certified tandem instructors by their sides, passengers are securely hitched to the hang gliders. The gliders are then towed up to more than 2000 feet behind a motorized ultralight. Once the instructor releases the tow line, adventurers enjoy views of the Valley and the Tennessee River from a totally new perspective. After just one introductory tandem flight, many brave souls often claim to feel more alive than they felt the day before!

Hunter Museum of American Art
Chattanooga, Tennessee

Overlooking the Tennessee River and located atop an 80-foot limestone bluff, the Hunter Museum of American Art is a haven for all art lovers. This is one of the most modern and attractive museums in the entire Tennessee Valley. The museum, adjacent

to the Bluff View Art District, is sectionalized by time periods. Displays range from *Early American Symbols* (1730-1850) to the *Pop Art* of today. The galleries are audience-centered, built with the intention of allowing visitors to define their own views of America. The lobby and special exhibitions sections are both roomy and attractive, and the facility was designed to encourage visitors to use the museum, instead of simply visit it. In addition to the special exhibitions section, the museum features permanent collection galleries, educational studios, and an auditorium for presentations to large groups. The building is actually an integration of two facilities: the original museum containing historical collections, and a modernistic west wing, which houses contemporary collections and temporary exhibitions. The museum also has a café and a store open during regular museum hours. There are volunteers stationed throughout the museum to assist visitors and answer questions pertaining to the numerous displays and collections. This unique museum provides one of the most engaging American history and sociology lessons available, and does so with one-of-a-kind paintings, sculptures, and other artistic creations.

* Tony Scherman (b. 1950), *Il Mostro*, 1998, encaustic on canvas, 84 x 96 inches, Hunter Museum of American Art, Chattanooga, Tennessee,
In honor of Julius L. Chazen, a gift of the Unus Foundation, Nanci & Steve Chazen and Jack Saks-Chazen

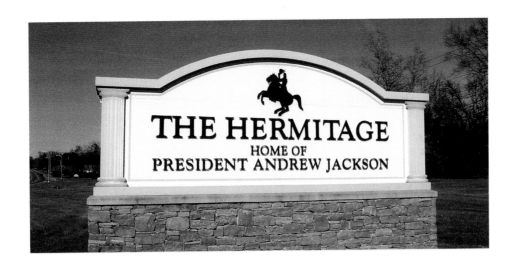

"One man with courage makes a majority."

Andrew Jackson

The Hermitage
Nashville, Tennessee

The Hermitage once served as home to Andrew "Old Hickory" Jackson, the seventh president of the United States. Prior to becoming president, Jackson was a prosecuting attorney, congressman, senator, military general (he was nicknamed "The Hero of New Orleans"), and the first territorial governor of Florida. Jackson eventually served as president from 1829 until 1837. The Hermitage consists of numerous buildings, gardens, a Confederate cemetery, and a church. It also features the tombs of Jackson and his wife, Rachel. At the time of Jackson's death in 1845, the property consisted of approximately 1,000 acres. In Jackson's day, about 140 slaves performed the wide range of tasks required to run the farm. The former plantation now features a biographical film on Jackson's life and an attractive museum displaying numerous artifacts. Guides in period costumes also conduct tours of the mansion. Except for major holidays and the third week of January, the Hermitage is open throughout the year.

CHAPTER VI:
Alabama Attractions and Locations Within the Valley
The Yellowhammer State

Alabama's nickname originated during the Civil War when a company of Huntsville-based Confederate soldiers arrived on the scene with brand new uniforms. These uniforms came complete with bright yellow armbands, much to the amusement of the other battle-weary troops. A soldier cried out, "Yellowhammer, Yellowhammer, flicker, flicker!" After the laughter died down, word soon traveled of the Alabama soldiers' new nickname. The yellowhammer is now, appropriately, Alabama's state bird.

Among Alabama's most noteworthy features are its contributions to the worlds of science, military defense, and space exploration. Huntsville is the proud home of Space Camp and the internationally known U.S. Space and Rocket Center. In addition, located within Redstone Arsenal is NASA's George C. Marshall Space Flight Center – responsible for developing and testing some of the largest booster engines in the world.

Alabama at a Glance

Statehood Admission:	December 14, 1819
State Bird:	Yellowhammer
State Flower:	Camelia
State Tree:	Longleaf Pine
Area:	52,423 sq. mi. (30th in U.S.)
Land:	50,750 sq. mi. (28th in U.S.)
Water:	1,673 sq. mi. (23rd in U.S.)
Coastline:	53 mi. (17th in U.S.)
Shoreline:	607 mi. (19th in U.S.)
Agriculture:	Poultry and eggs, cattle, nursery stock, peanuts, cotton, vegetables, milk, soybeans
Industry:	Paper, lumber and wood products, mining, rubber and plastic products, transportation equipment, apparel
Geographic Center:	12 miles southwest of Clanton
Population:	4,447,100
Persons per sq. mile:	87.6
State Name Origin:	Named after Creek Indian word for "tribal town"

Natural beauty in its finest form can be seen from high atop Gorham's Bluff (near Pisgah) and from down below, deep inside Grant's Cathedral Caverns. North Alabama has a multitude of beautiful lakes, lush forests, and scenic hiking trails. It is also known for its wildlife. Hunting and fishing are both popular in this state, as is bird watching.

A few weekends of travel throughout north Alabama, and you will find it has been home to many of our country's most impressive and colorful personalities. We can draw inspiration from the home of the deaf and blind girl who went on to lecture around the world, or from photos of the African-American sprinter whose civil rights aspirations extended well beyond winning Olympic gold medals. Impressive religious structures can also be found just a short drive away from astounding technological ones.

Not every attraction in this region is a powerful, awe-inspiring spectacle, however. Sometimes being odd and unique can be more than enough! Take, for instance, the Coon Dog Cemetery in Cherokee, or Scottsboro's Unclaimed Baggage Center.

As this chapter will show you, northern Alabama has a great deal to offer. And don't forget, if you read about an attraction you simply must visit, the directory at the end of this book provides contact information.

"What has always been clear, for Southerner and non-Southerner alike, is that Dixie is the most fascinating part of the country. There may be a book out there called 'The Great Midwest' or 'A Turn in the Midwest' or 'The Mind of the Midwest' or 'The Midwestern Mystique,' but if there is I'm certainly not aware of it."

Fred Hobson, Ph.D.
Southern Author

Introduction to North Alabama
Cradle of the Valley

It is undisputed that northern California is completely different than southern California. When compared to other parts of Alabama, can the same be said of north Alabama? Many believe northern Alabama constitutes a "state within a state." It is a unique area where the mountains meet the magnolias. The southern part of the Tennessee Valley – both north and south of the southern "hook" of the Tennessee River – has its roots in cultural contrasts. The people living in this part of the Valley reflect backgrounds, dialects, and cultures from many parts of the nation as well as foreign countries. Its geography is also varied, ranging from beautiful mountains in the east of the state, to cotton fields in the middle, to lakes and rolling rivers in the west. The Appalachian foothills begin in north Alabama. It is an area where mammoth rockets are tested and bald eagles soar. Fishing, hiking, and recreation trails are common throughout the region. Camping, boating, and golf are as popular here as they are anywhere in the South.

From outdoor adventures to cultural experiences, there are endless opportunities to explore. History, musical legends, and Indian artifacts are very much alive here. It is also an area with intense state-of-the-art scientific development pioneered by some of the nation's largest corporations. You only need to visit this area to better understand why it has become so popular with residents and tourists alike.

A visit to north Alabama may include journeys to small towns frozen in time. Many pleasant afternoons can be spent in these destinations, walking through historical areas proud of their past. Meeting local storekeepers and residents is always an adventure you don't want to miss. You can also find Victorian homes throughout the area dating back to the early 1800s as well as Civil War memorials. A leisurely drive south of the Tennessee River brings you to Gadsden and Cullman. Gadsden is known for Noccalula Falls Park as well as its industrial center and rich Cherokee and early-settler heritage. You will undoubtedly enjoy Cullman's German heritage as well as a visit to Ave Maria Grotto located on the grounds of a Benedictine monastery. The local flea market and museum should not be missed. Both of these north Alabama cities symbolize growing and progressive communities symbolic of the new South.

Although they do not share the reputations as tourist meccas that Nashville or Chattanooga do, the major northern Alabama cities (Huntsville/Madison, Decatur, and those in the Shoals area) are dynamic in many ways. Starting in 1802 with the construction of a cabin by John Hunt near a big spring, Huntsville and the surrounding area eventually became an important cotton trading center and a rail transportation hub. In the 1950s, Wernher von Braun and his team of German scientists designed and tested rockets in Huntsville that put man on the moon. Since then, the area has become an international military and civilian leader in software and aerospace development.

City leaders boast that according to the latest U.S. census, the area has the highest per capita rate of engineers in the nation. Thousands of companies, including numerous *Fortune* 500 firms, have migrated to the region, and Madison County now consists of a population of more than 276,000. While other modern cities such as Houston, Texas, and Cape Canaveral, Florida, point to their aerospace and high-tech image, Huntsville is truly unique in one respect. It is one of the leading, state-of-the-art cities in the nation that also prides itself on its wealthy historical background and on being the site of the state's first constitutional convention. History and the future are truly intertwined in this dynamic city.

"North Alabama offers so much to residents and visitors alike.

The natural beauty of the foothills of the Appalachians combined with the

Tennessee River make the area ideal for a wide variety of activities. The

variety and number of attractions in North Alabama is outstanding and the hospitality

of the people is second to none. This area has the perfect combination of

Old South charm and history blended with 21st-century, cutting-edge technology."

Judy Ryals
President/CEO
Huntsville/Madison County Convention & Visitors Bureau

Decatur has grown from an early 1800s village along the Tennessee River to a modern city with a population of 56,000. It is home to one of the largest "open bay" high-tech industrial facilities in the country – Boeing's 1.4 million-square-foot plant, which manufactures the huge Delta II and Delta IV rockets. Decatur is also a city of history, touting Alabama's largest Victorian-era historic district. The old Decatur historic district encompasses more than 116 acres, with houses built as early as 1829. There are excellent walking tours within the area. With nearby Athens to the north and Hartselle to the south, Decatur is a growing community with a small-town feel.

The scenic northwest region of the state – consisting of Florence, Muscle Shoals, Sheffield, Tuscumbia, and two counties (Lauderdale and Colbert) – comprise what is locally known as "The Shoals." It is literally a "tale of four cities" with a history ranging from the mystical legacy of Indian tribes to the heritage of soul and country music, much of which originated here. TVA's dams, lakes and reservoirs built since the mid-1930s have made this part of the state a haven for water sports enthusiasts. Be it recreation or commerce, the entire Shoals area offers the experience of small Southern towns with the amenities of large cities.

CITY OF FLORENCE

Florence was surveyed for the Cypress Land Company in 1818 by Ferdinand Sannoner and named for the famous capital of Tuscany. The county seat of Lauderdale County, it was first incorporated in 1826. Located at the foot of Muscle Shoals, it became a thriving agricultural and commercial center with light industry and significant religious, educational, and medical institutions. During the Civil War, Florence was occupied by both armies at various times. The Tennessee Valley Authority with Wilson and Wheeler Dams contributed to further economic development.

The issue is not whether you can find something of interest in north Alabama, but whether you wish to venture out and explore the wonderful adventures and opportunities surrounding you. The decision is yours.

Exploring Huntsville –
A Brief Journey Through History
Huntsville, Alabama

EarlyWorks Children's Museum

The EarlyWorks Children's Museum, advertised as the South's largest children's "hands-on" history museum, is located around the corner from Alabama's Constitution Village. This state-of-the-art museum, which is divided into numerous rooms and halls, provides a myriad of activities and educational experiences for children of all ages. It contains a theater which regularly shows the film *Alabama: From Territory to Statehood*. The museum provides basic lessons on Alabama's river life, as well as period clothing, music, and folklore. Some of the more unique exhibits include a 16-foot floor map, a talking tree, a 46-foot keelboat, and a Hall of Presidents which details the lives and times of America's foremost leaders. Families and groups are welcome throughout the year.

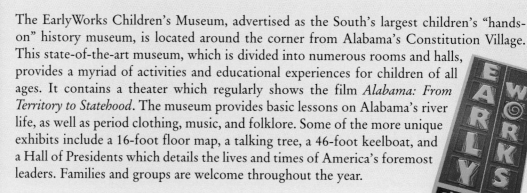

Huntsville Railroad Depot and Museum

Located approximately one mile from the Madison County Courthouse, this depot is one of the country's oldest remaining railroad structures. Built in 1860 as part of the Memphis & Charleston Railroad, the depot was soon taken over by the Union Army in the early part of the Civil War. Confederate prisoners were kept here, and you can still see their graffiti written on three walls of the upper story. The depot – which is part of the EarlyWorks Complex – contains several buildings, locomotives, and other rolling stock and has a large model railroad located in its main exhibit hall. The depot also features rooms displaying detailed replicas of railroad workers and their offices. On the upper floors, detailed Civil War relics, memorabilia, and exhibits illustrate some of the challenges Union and Confederate troops alike endured during the war.

Constitution Village

Considered the "Birthplace of Alabama," Constitution Village is a vivid reconstruction of what Huntsville was like when delegates gathered here in 1819 to write the state's first constitution. The village has four main buildings and seven out-buildings filled with early 19th-century furnishings symbolic of the times. The buildings, however, are only a small part of the attraction. Interpreters in period clothing lead you back into history while performing many of the same daily tasks of the state's first citizens. Depending on the time of year, you can spot reenactors dipping candles, smoking meats, picking cotton bolls, dyeing textiles, weaving baskets, brewing beer, building cabinets, and making lye soap. If you have an appetite, the grounds include a confectionary shop with freshly baked goods and candies. Unique crafts and souvenirs are available for purchase as well.

SITE–ALABAMA'S FIRST CONSTITUTIONAL CONVENTION

Here, on July 5, 1819 forty-four delegates from twenty-two Counties in the Alabama Territory met to frame a State Constitution which was accepted and signed August 2, 1819. Convention leadership was furnished by two Huntsvillians, John Williams Walker, president, and Clement Comer Clay, chairman of a committee appointed to draft the document.

Weeden House Museum

The Weeden House Museum, located one block from Constitution Village in the Twickenham Historic District, was built in 1819. It was purchased in 1845 by Dr. William Weeden, but was later requisitioned for use by Federal officers during the Civil War. The white two-story brick home was the birthplace of poet/artist Maria Howard Weeden (1847-1905) and the present home to 20 of her paintings. She is known for her watercolor paintings of 19th-century African-Americans and her poetry, which was eloquently written in the ethnic vernacular of the times. Copies of many of these works are for sale at the museum. Furnished with period antiques from the mid-1800s, the house is owned by the city of Huntsville and leased by the Twickenham Historic Preservation District Association.

Harrison Brothers Hardware

Placed on the National Register of Historic Places in 1980, this building is much more than just a hardware store. It is a living, breathing landmark which was established in 1879, and remains a shopper's and visitor's delight. You can find goods and curiosities from times gone by, recalling childhood memories. The store is stocked from floorboard to high ceiling with old-fashioned tools, nostalgic hardware, housewares, local crafts, and some of the most interesting souvenirs imaginable. Located on Huntsville's courthouse square, Harrison Brothers is owned and operated by the Historic Huntsville Foundation.

HARRISON BROTHERS HARDWARE
Established 1879

Harrison Brothers, the oldest operating hardware store in Alabama, was founded in 1879 when James B. and Daniel T. Harrison opened a tobacco shop on Jefferson Street. In 1897 they purchased this building on South Side Square and expanded into the adjoinin building in 1902. Both buildings were remodeled following a 1901 fire, but alterations since then have been minimal. The brothers' stock evolved from tobacco through crockery, furniture, jewelry, appliances and finally into hardware. Two generations of Harrisons ran the business before it was bought in 1984 as a preservation project by the non-profit Historic Huntsville Foundation which operates it today. The buildings were listed on the National Register of Historic Places in 1980.

Alabama Music Hall of Fame
Tuscumbia, Alabama

Every state in America boasts of its musical stars and composers and Alabama is no exception. This state, however, is somewhat unique in that it does not lay claim to any one type of music. Alabamians have impressively contributed to rock, classical, country and western, rhythm and blues, gospel, soul, and plenty of styles in between. At the Alabama Music Hall of Fame, you can relish the memories and music inspired by Hank Williams, Alabama, Tammy Wynette, Lionel Richie, Nat "King" Cole, and hundreds of other top-named artists. Muscle Shoals, the early home of W.C. Handy – known as the "Father of the Blues" – hails as the birthplace of numerous musical stars and songwriters alike. Regardless of your musical tastes, if you enjoy music, you'll want to visit this state-of-the-art facility, which proudly displays artists and their music. Each August, the Alabama Music Hall of Fame holds an outdoor concert called the "Harvest Jam," drawing thousands of music buffs from around the country.

Burritt
on the Mountain
Huntsville, Alabama

Located just outside of Huntsville atop Monte Sano Mountain, Burritt on the Mountain is a place for recreation, reflection, and education. It was bequeathed to the city in 1955 by Dr. William Burritt. Today, this site is an institution with many faces. It contains a mansion, a "living museum," and a history park. The mansion was built in 1936, and has two rooms adorned with original furnishings. The museum, listed in the National Register of Historic Places, has exhibit galleries of local and regional interest. The historic park is complete with 19th-century farmsteads, barnyard animals (goats, sheep, chickens, rabbits, etc.), and crops, and has informative, daily displays of how the early farmers lived. It also features many hands-on exhibits and demonstrations, with staff dressed in period costumes performing a variety of that era's daily chores. This location also features locally supported educational

history programs, which are enjoyable for family members of all ages. The adjacent walking trails on the property overlook the city of Huntsville. The museum publishes a calendar of events containing a listing of the numerous concerts, tours, singing groups, and Christmas activities held at this beautiful and relaxing location.

Covered Bridges
of Blount County
Blount County, Alabama

While many people look for exciting festivals and events on weekends, others seek out more traditional attractions found by way of the road less traveled. In Blount County, near Oneonta, three of the state's 13 covered bridges remain. Blount County is Alabama's official "Covered Bridge Capital." The Easley Bridge is the oldest and measures 95 feet across. The bridge is a single-span structure built in 1927, and remains in very good condition. The Horton Mill Bridge was constructed in 1933, and is 220 feet long. It is listed in the National Register of Historic Places, and is reputed to be higher (70 feet above the Black Warrior River) than any other covered bridge in the United States. Third on the list is Swann Bridge, built around 1935. This three-span bridge is 324 feet in length and spans the Locust Fork on the Warrior River. It is the longest covered bridge still in existence in the state. All three bridges remain in use today. The Covered Bridge Festival, held each October, features bridge tours and arts-and-crafts exhibits.

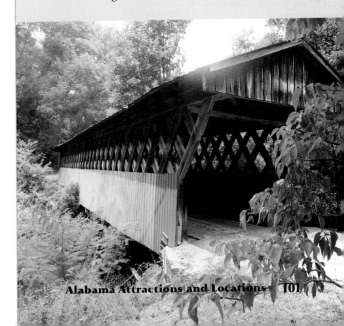

Shrine of the Most Blessed Sacrament
Hanceville, Alabama

In 1995, while on a trip to Bogota, Columbia, Mother M. Angelica had a religious vision. She promptly returned to Hanceville and proceeded to spearhead the construction of a magnificent complex that would attract worshippers from around the globe. The

Shrine and Piazza were constructed between 1997 and 1999 on an isolated piece of farmland outside Hanceville, off Interstate 65. Materials for the Shrine were imported from all over the world, as were the artisans and craftsmen who custom designed the many rooms, statutes, and altars. The Shrine features Romanesque-Gothic architecture that was heavily influenced by the Franciscan churches and monasteries of 13th-century Assisi. In early 2000, construction began on Castle San Miguel, which houses a gift shop, a conference center, eating areas, and offices. Near the castle is a devotional chapel containing a near life-size Nativity scene. The Shrine is open to the public daily, and worshippers are encouraged to attend both Mass and confession.

"I know there is something very special here. The fruit of it, we don't know. But everyone who comes in is very aware of the presence of the Father, the Son, and the Holy Spirit."
Mother M. Angelica

Old State
Bank Building
Decatur, Alabama

Because the Memphis and Charleston Railroad crossed the Tennessee River in north Alabama at Decatur, this city became a strategic location for the South during the latter years of the Civil War. The town eventually became the focus of a fierce four-day battle – both on land and river – between advancing Confederates and garrisoned Union troops. The entire city was destroyed except for four buildings, one of which was the Old State Bank (which was also used as a hospital during that period). This pre-Greek revival structure is the oldest bank in the state. It features an 1830s-period re-creation of what the facility used to look like and how it operated. The building is open on weekends by appointment and during regular business hours during the week.

Fort Payne Depot Museum
Fort Payne, Alabama

A visit to the Depot Museum is a venture into nostalgia. The Fort Payne Depot was built in 1891 by the Alabama Great Southern Railroad and served as the community's passenger station until 1970. Built of pink sandstone, the Richardsonian Romanesque-style structure presents numerous exhibits showcasing lifestyles of the 1800s and early 1900s. It displays Native American artifacts of the Cherokee, Hopi, Apache, Seminole, and Pueblo tribes. Pottery, basketry, weapons, and clothing are just a few of the interesting items you can study. You can also find a player piano, a fantastic collection of antique dioramas (three-dimensional picture boxes), railroad memorabilia, Civil War relics, and numerous photographs throughout the building. A tour of this museum gives you a better impression of what life was like many years ago.

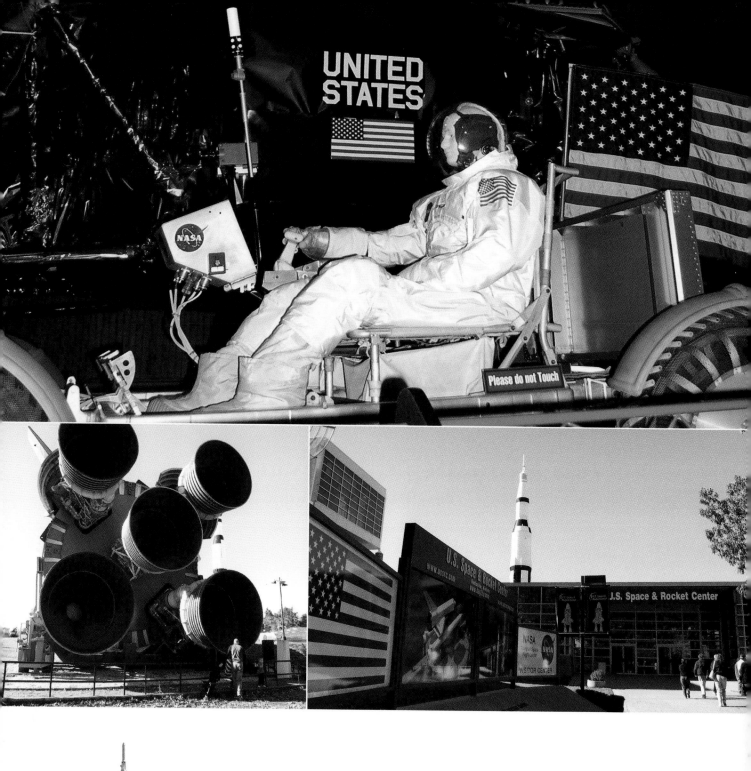

"The world's largest space attraction features dozens of interactive exhibits surrounding Apollo, Mercury and Space Shuttle spacecraft. The U.S. Space and Rocket Center is the only place in the world where you can stand under a 'full stack' – the Space Shuttle, external tank and two rocket boosters."

Al Whitaker
Media Relations Manager
U.S. Space and Rocket Center

U.S. Space and Rocket Center
Huntsville, Alabama

Listed as the top tourist attraction in Alabama, the U.S. Space and Rocket Center is also one of the most popular family attractions within the Tennessee Valley. Located directly off Interstate 565 west of Huntsville, the Center promises a full day of adventure and education for both young and old. Outside the Center, enjoy numerous exhibits, such as Rocket Park, which features replicas of full-scale rockets. The Space and Rocket Center proudly displays a space shuttle mounted atop an external tank and two solid rocket boosters, as well as an SR-71 Blackbird, the spy plane that flew coast-to-coast in under 68 minutes. Nearby is a national historic landmark – the 363-foot Saturn V rocket designed in Huntsville to take astronauts to the moon. The truly adventurous are welcome to strap into the Space Shot Simulator, an exhilarating vertical thrill ride. Inside the Center there are numerous rooms discussing the history of rocketry and the beginning of the National Aeronautics and Space Administration – NASA. The museum features hands-on exhibits as well as a Space Walk simulator, an Apollo Cockpit Trainer, a G-Force Accelerator, and many pictures and videos of pioneers of space travel. You also have the opportunity to view an IMAX film in the Spacedome Theater. The Center, also the home of U.S. Space Camp and the Aviation Challenge, is adjacent to Redstone Arsenal and the George C. Marshall Space Flight Center. As museums go, this one is as entertaining as it is informative.

"Why stay attached to the earth? The moon is so close by."

Herman Oberth
"The Father of Space Travel"

Skydiving in the Valley
Cullman, Alabama

Museums aren't for everybody. Skydive Alabama, Cullman's very own skydiving operation, caters to those thrill seekers who just refuse to settle for entertainment below 14,000 feet. First-time jumpers (who jump tandem with nationally-certified instructors) are always welcome to go up with the seasoned soloists. Newbies flying tandem even get to help steer their parachute! Comprehensive training is offered for those who wish to make the jump from timid novice to crackerjack expert. Helmet-mounted video and still photography are also available (and recommended, if only for bragging rights down the road).

Ivy Green
The Birthplace of Helen Keller
Tuscumbia, Alabama

The Keller home, built in 1820 on a 640-acre tract in Tuscumbia, is listed in the National Register of Historic Places. To many, this home is more than just a location, it is an inspiring monument to human accomplishment and courage. Nineteen months after Helen Keller was born here, she was stricken with a severe illness that left her not only mute, but also blind *and* deaf. The home contains many of the Keller family's original furniture pieces and hundreds of mementos of Helen's life, including her library of Braille books and an old Braille typewriter. The home reflects the education of a woman who was eventually nicknamed "America's First Lady of Courage." Keller went on to become a noted traveler who lectured in more than 25 countries. The incredible story is re-created in *The Miracle Worker,* an annual production held on the grounds every summer. The Helen Keller Festival is held for one week during this period at Tuscumbia's Spring Park.

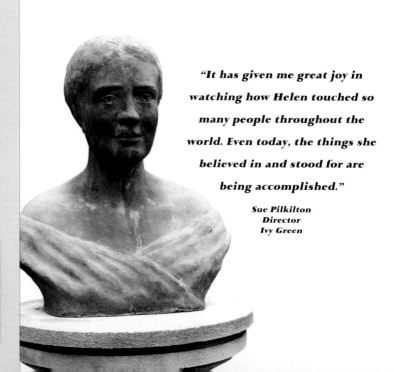

"It has given me great joy in watching how Helen touched so many people throughout the world. Even today, the things she believed in and stood for are being accomplished."

**Sue Pilkilton
Director
Ivy Green**

* Top photograph courtesy of *Skydive Alabama,* Chris Harwell, 2006

Gorham's Bluff

Pisgah, Alabama

Overlooking the Tennessee River valley, a unique community sits high atop Sand Mountain, near Pisgah. The developers of this area are building a town on a 160-acre site dedicated to the preservation of local natural beauty and the arts. In addition to constructing numerous attractive homes and cottages, the town is slowly expanding to include a pavilion, a meeting house, and an amphitheater. The location of these facilities inspires almost all who come to either participate directly in one of numerous events held throughout the year or to simply appreciate the artistic productions performed there. One of the leading proponents of the movement is the Gorham's Bluff Institute. Created in 1994, this nonprofit organization is dedicated to providing a wide variety of artistic and educational activities to the public. Currently, some of the major festivals presented by the Institute include the Storytelling Festival in May, the Gerhart Chamber Music Festival in June, the Alabama Ballet Summer Residency in July, and the Summer Theatre Festival in August. These events are supplemented by various musical performances and other cultural events for all members of the family. Particularly noteworthy is the Gorham's Bluff Lodge, located on the edge of the bluff. This location provides a breathtaking view of the Valley. The atmosphere and beauty of Gorham's Bluff is truly a reflection of Southern charm at its finest.

Wheeler National Wildlife Refuge
Decatur, Alabama

Located along the Tennessee River between Decatur and Huntsville, this attraction is divided into two sections – the visitor center and the refuge. The main building is a modern, 10,000-square-foot interpretative center, featuring wildlife displays of the species inhabiting the refuge and nearby area. The visitor center, operated by the U.S. Fish and Wildlife Service, has an informative orientation video for the entire family. The building is within walking distance of two hiking trails as well as a unique wildlife observation building. The observation building is a great location to view the numerous species of wildlife during both winter and summer. The center itself backs up to a 35,000-acre refuge, which is home to more than 500 species of wildlife and provides many opportunities for outdoor recreation.

Coon Dog Cemetery
Colbert County, Alabama

Only in Alabama! This cemetery, located just south of Cherokee, was started in 1937 when a famous coon dog named Troop was buried with full honors. Located in the heart of hunting country near a large hunting camp, this cemetery now contains more than 100 tombstones and markers dedicated to man's best friend. Many of the tombstones feature personalized epitaphs, which make for interesting reading. Every Labor Day, Cherokee throws a festival to honor the dogs, a celebration that includes bluegrass music and buck dancing.

Only Cemetery of Its Kind In The World
ONLY COON HOUNDS ARE ALLOWED TO BE BURIED.
TROOP First Dog Laid To Rest Here Sept. 4, 1937
Please Be Careful With Fire!

"All dogs go to heaven."

Unknown

Cathedral Caverns
Grant, Alabama

Originally called Bat's Cave, Cathedral Caverns was purchased and opened to the public by Jacob Gurley in 1955. When his wife entered the caverns for the first time, she remarked that the impressive high walls with their stalactites and stalagmites resembled

the interior of a cathedral. The walking tour of the caverns in this 461-acre state park (14 of which are composed of caves) lasts about an hour and a half. Over the course of these 90 minutes, you will see prehistoric shark teeth, bats, stalagmite forests, and unique natural beauty. The caverns feature a record-breaking, 45-foot-tall stalagmite with a circumference of 243 feet (named *Goliath*, appropriately enough). The cave's entrance holds a world's record of its own, measuring a breathtaking 126 feet at its widest point and 25 feet at its highest. The inside of the caverns is dramatically lit with more than 40 miles of wiring, using 80,000 watts. The guide provides an informative, and at the same time thoroughly entertaining, "down home" history and science lesson. Admission is dirt cheap, and people of all ages find the formations to be magnificent. Featured curiosities include *Big Rock Canyon, Mystery River,* and *Stalagmite Mountain.* Due to its constant 60 degree temperature, you can enjoy this attraction year-round. Cathedral Caverns was featured in the 1995 Disney film *Tom and Huck,* but seeing it in person is a much more intense experience!

"Awesome. Coolest hole in the ground I ever been to."

Jeremy Saint
Caverns Visitor

4 WORLD RECORDS

Ave Maria Grotto
Cullman, Alabama

Architecture students, fans of gingerbread houses, and amateur sandcastle engineers will all enjoy a trip to this one-of-a-kind curiosity. Opened in 1934, the Grotto is located on the grounds of the St. Bernard Abbey – the only Benedictine monastery in Alabama. Listed on the National Register of Historic Places, it consists of a four-acre landscaped hillside of stone and cement structures. These are the handiwork of Brother Joseph Zoettl, a monk who lived at the Abbey for almost 70 years. Feel free to venture out on a self-guided tour to view more than 125 miniature replicas of biblical structures and world-famous buildings. Sculptures ranging from the ancient city of Jerusalem to Bavarian folklore scenes have been intricately carved into this former stone quarry.

Pope's Museum and Tavern
Florence, Alabama

This building has seen many owners and has served many purposes. Built in the 1800s, it is located on what was known as Jackson's Military Road and became an early center for commerce. It was also a stagecoach stop, a tavern, and an inn. General Andrew Jackson traveled this road on his march to battle the British in New Orleans. It was once used as a hospital by both the Confederate and Union forces during the Civil War. Owned by the city of Florence, it is now an attractive museum housing a wealth of local history and pioneer artifacts that reflect the style of the early settler's life. The museum holds an annual Frontier Day Celebration the first weekend of every June. If you are exploring the Shoals, this is well worth a visit.

Oakville Indian Mounds Education Center
Danville, Alabama

If you're interested in Tennesseee Valley Indians, don't miss the Oakville Indian Mounds Education Center, located eight miles southeast of Moulton. The Center contains a park, an early settler's cemetery, a Copena Indian burial mound and a massive 2,000-year-old, 27-foot high ceremonial mound that is the largest woodland mound in Alabama. Nearby stands a modern, seven-sided museum, which is an 8,000-square-foot replica of a Cherokee council house. Inside the building is one of the best collections of Indian artifacts in the Tennessee Valley, many of which date as far back as 10,000 B.C. In the center of the museum stands a wooden 12-foot statute of Sequoyah, who developed the Cherokee alphabet for his tribe.

CHEROKEE COUNCIL HOUSE MUSEUM

The Oakville Indian Mounds Museum is based on a seven sided Cherokee council house. This type of council house was used during the cooler months and an open sided rectangular pavilion during warmer weather. The descriptions used for the museum's construction came from Lt. Henry Timberlake, who visited the Cherokee capitol at Chota in 1761, and William Bartram, who visited Cowe about 1765. Timberlake's description: "The townhouse, in which are transacted all public business and diversions, is raised with wood, and covered over with earth, and has all the appearance of a small mountain at a little distance. It is built in the form of a sugar loaf, and large enough to contain 500 persons, but extremely dark, having, besides the door, which is narrow that but one at a time can pass, and that after much winding and turning, but one small aperture to let the smoke out, which is so ill contrived, that most of it settles in the ancient amphitheater, the seats being raised one above another, leaving an area in the middle, in the center of which stands the fire; the seats of the head warriors are nearest it." The seven sides represent the matrilineal clans of the Cherokee: Wild Potato, Long Hair, Paint, Wolf, Deer, Bird, and Blue.

The Dismals
Phil Campbell, Alabama

The Dismals (also known as Dismals Canyon) showcases examples of the ecological and geological formations that contribute to our region's natural history. This unique park is located near Phil Campbell, approximately 12 miles south of Russellville, Alabama. The canyon has the distinction of being home to tiny glow-in-the-dark creatures known as "dismalites." The only other known location of these phosphorescent anomalies is New Zealand! The canyon itself is comprised of caves, natural grottos, rock bridges, waterfalls, bluffs, and narrow passageways. Designated as a Registered Natural Landmark in 1975 by the National Park Service, the canyon features a one-mile walk with views of Indian ceremonial grounds. This is a very clean and uncrowded place to visit. It offers hiking challenges and first-hand opportunities to get in touch with the natural beauty that the Tennessee Valley has to offer.

Cook's Science Museum
Decatur, Alabama

Learning *can* be fun, we promise! This museum in Decatur, Alabama, allows adults and children alike to explore the natural wonders of the world with habitats, hands-on exhibits, and interactive displays. Cook's features a vast collection of wildlife and sealife alike. It contains rare displays of many of earth's creatures, including a bald eagle and a golden eagle, as well as many species of insects. It has a 64-seat auditorium, which often hosts science presentations to school children, civic organizations, and church groups. The museum also features a variety of gifts and souvenirs from this unique educational facility.

Jesse Owens Memorial Park
Oakville, Alabama

The Tennessee Valley is home to its share of heroes. One of those heroes is remembered and celebrated near Oakville, Alabama. The Jesse Owens Memorial Park contains a welcome center, ball fields, picnic pavilions, and an attractive museum. You can trace the path of this African-American sharecropper's son from grade school through to his successful career both as a sports figure and business leader in youth sports programs. The park also features an impressive photo display of various moments of Jesse's life. One enjoyable movie clip shows Jesse Owens winning four gold metals at the 1936 Olympic Games in Berlin, Germany, much to the dismay of Chancellor Adolf Hitler. Owens won the gold in the 100-meter dash, the 200-meter dash, the broad jump, and as a member of the 400-meter relay team. He was the first American track-and-fielder to win four gold medals in a single Olympics. In 1976, Jesse was awarded the Medal of Freedom (the highest honor a United States civilian can receive) by President Gerald Ford. A visit to this museum can provide an enjoyable afternoon, with an inspiring history lesson to boot.

"The man who humbled Hitler."

American Expression

Little River Canyon National Preserve
DeKalb and Cherokee Counties, Alabama

This preserve is in northeastern Alabama near Interstate 59 and Fort Payne, Alabama. Simply put, this lesser-known park is one of the real beauties of the Tennessee Valley. It contains one of the nation's longest mountaintop rivers – Little River. The river forms and flows for most of its length atop the mountain, then plunges off the Cumberland Plateau and eventually flows into Weiss Lake. The canyon is the largest and one of the deepest chasms east of the Mississippi River and provides a breathtaking view of water-falls, rivers, and overlooks. Added to the National Park System in 1992, the Preserve has something for everyone. If you are in search of a challenge, Little River National Preserve offers canoeing, mountain-bike riding, camping, and horseback riding. For you extreme thrill seekers, rock climbing, white-water rafting, and kayaking are also available. Waterways range from from laid-back Class I rapids to expert Class VI rapids. If you are interested in natural beauty, you will enjoy scenic overlooks, hiking opportunities, day-use areas, and the beautiful Canyon Rim Drive. Desoto State Park is also located within the Preserve's boundaries. This park provides everything a weekend warrior would need for a wonderful family mini-vacation. Before you plan a far away trip in search of new scenery, consider visiting this hidden, well-preserved local destination.

North Alabama Birding Trail
Throughout North Alabama

When the average person thinks of a birding trail, he or she often envisions a footpath in a remote woodland, where environmental groups endlessly search for rare birds. If you share that perspective, consider familiarizing yourself with the North Alabama Birding Trail. This attraction, covering 50 sites throughout north Alabama, opened in the fall of 2005 and is sponsored and funded by the Alabama Department of Conservation and Natural Resources and a host of other state, local, federal, and private organizations.

Within the five major bird groups – birds of prey, waterfowl, shorebirds, wading birds, and songbirds – there are hundreds of species that populate this area. The well-marked sites and inter-pretative kiosks throughout the trail provide a substantial source of information. These kiosks, with images and descriptions of the birds, offer information about both the long-term feath-ered residents and the short-term feathered visitors.

A free brochure about the trail provides bird watchers with pictures of many of our regional birds and divides the area into three geographical sections. The Northwest Loop has 15 sites, including such areas as Wheeler, Wilson, and Pickwick lakes, Bankhead National Forest, and the Natchez Trace. The Central Loop has 18 sites, which include areas such as the Wheeler National Wildlife Refuge, Monte Sano State Park, and Hurricane Creek Park. The Northeast Loop identifies 17 sites along the more mountainous portion of the state. This loop includes such tourist attractions as Guntersville Lake, Little River Canyon National Preserve, Buck's Pocket, and Gorham's Bluff. The visitor guide contains a north Alabama map identifying all sites, global positioning system (GPS) coordinates, specific driving instructions, and beautiful pictures of the birds indigenous to the area. The group of sponsoring organizations hold an annual birding festival in late spring. Whether you're interested in a major birding exploration or just a quiet morning walk, once you have the visitor guide to locate these areas, you have no excuse not to pull on a pair of hiking boots and take off!

Jerry Brown Pottery
Hamilton, Alabama

For nine generations, Jerry Brown's family has been transforming local clay into works of household art. Jerry's pottery pieces, particularly his quirky face jugs, have attracted nationwide attention, appearing in such magazines as *Southern Living* and *Good Housekeeping*. A visit to Jerry's studio in Hamilton quickly becomes a lesson in the nuts and bolts of pottery-making. From digging up and grinding the clay with the assistance of a mule, to sculpting and firing of the pieces – it all culminates into uniquely beautiful artwork. This insightful location is more than just a display studio. Jerry and his wife, Sandra, are eager to explain the process and will encourage you to sit and watch Jerry as he spins new pieces on the pottery wheel. Moonshine and vinegar jugs, egg separators, chicken cookers, and numerous other pieces of kitchenware are available in a variety of splendid colors and finishes. Jerry has pieces on display in galleries as far away as Israel, and now even has his own festival, which takes place the first weekend in March. For what may be the most interesting souvenirs found in the region, consider an informative visit to Jerry's studio.

Russell Cave National Monument
Bridgeport, Alabama

On May 11, 1961, President John F. Kennedy dedicated this location as a national monument, and its visitor center was soon to follow in 1967. The rock from which Russell Cave was naturally hollowed was formed more than 300 million years ago. It provides a very impressive tunnel entrance for those who want to learn about the geography and the early inhabitants of the area. The federal enclave consists of approximately 310 acres and provides insight into why this cave served as a refuge against the elements. Early travelers made their way through this area about 9,000 years ago. Used both as a burial ground and a hunting camp, the cave was first excavated in 1953. Many of the archeological findings, artifacts, weapons, and tools are preserved in the visitor center. The center hosts a Native American Indian Festival and conducts Junior Ranger Programs and other events throughout the year. Russell Cave National Monument is located six miles from Bridgeport, Alabama.

Take a Dam Vacation
Alabama and Tennessee

If you're looking for something to do with the family over a weekend that would be educational, inexpensive, and out of the ordinary, you should consider exploring some of the many dams in the area. After September 11, 2001, federal dam structures were placed off-limits to the general public. However, many visitor centers are still open. These centers explain how electricity is created, and visitors can study the functions of penstocks,

turbines, electromagnets, and huge generators. You will also learn that in addition to hydroelectric-power production, the dams and facilities play critical roles in flood control, river navigation, irrigation, water quality, recreation, and economic growth. Throughout Tennessee and Alabama, there are numerous state and federal dam reservoirs that provide campgrounds, hiking trails, and a great deal of entertaining, recreational activities for travelers. The Tennessee Valley Authority (TVA) is an independent U.S. government corporate agency, created in 1933 by an act of Congress. Supported by the Army Corps of Engineers, the TVA controls a 650-mile navigation channel, which spans the entire length of the Tennessee River. It provides for the integrated development of the entire Tennessee River basin, an area of about 41,000 square miles. Its total area covers parts of seven states and provides electricity for 8.5 million residents. The complete hydroelectric system of the TVA includes some 50 dams and 47 reservoirs. Check them out!

Huntsville Museum of Art
Huntsville, Alabama

Located in beautiful Big Spring International Park, the Huntsville Museum of Art is considered north Alabama's leading visual arts center. It contains seven large galleries that present a variety of exhibitions throughout the year. Named as one of the state's *Top 10 Destinations* by the Alabama Bureau of Tourism and Travel, the museum regularly displays exhibits from its own 2,500-piece permanent collection. But the museum offers much more than art simply hanging on the walls! The museum also conducts gallery walks with artists and offers lectures, films, concerts, and other events on a regular basis. The museum features a gift shop offering a variety of unique art merchandise and an Art Reference Library located on its second floor. Complete your experience by enjoying lunch or dinner in the museum restaurant. The Huntsville Museum of Art is gaining a well-earned reputation throughout the South for bringing high-caliber touring exhibitions to the Tennessee Valley region. The wide variety of works created by nationally and regionally acclaimed artists provide a wonderful treat of culture, artistry, and imagination.

"The Huntsville Museum offers so much more than beautiful art.

You can spend an entire afternoon here with your family and friends."

Georgina Chapman
Communications Manager

* Emily Wilson (b. 1959, Memphis, TN) *Back from Heaven*, 1990, Wood, 34 x 40 x 2.5 inches, Purchased with funds provided by the Huntsville Museum Association, Image provided courtesy of the Huntsville Museum of Art
** David Parrish (b. 1939, Birmingham, AL) *Sunrise*, 1986, oil on canvas, 48 x 72 inches, Purchased with funds provided by the Women's Guild of the Huntsville Museum of Art, Image provided courtesy of the Huntsville Museum of Art

Bankhead National Forest
Lawrence and Winston Counties, Alabama

Located south of Moulton in northwest Alabama lies one of the South's finest deep woods. The area, first declared a national forest in 1918 by President Woodrow Wilson, has approximately 180,000 acres, much of it challenging terrain to novice hikers. Once you leave the perimeter roads, you will find yourself in rustic woodlands and tracks that contribute to the most primitive of adventure hikes. The national forest consists of numerous campgrounds, thousands of acres of water, and horseback riding, hiking, and bicycling trails. Within its boundaries, you can find four scenic campgrounds – Houston, Corinth, Clear Creek, and Brushy Lake – and plenty of picnic areas. In the middle of Bankhead Forest lies the 25,000-acre Sipsey Wilderness, which has Alabama's only nationally-designated wild and scenic river – the Sipsey Fork. The Sipsey features beautiful canoeing streams and is one of the most pristine, untouched camping areas in the South. One-third of the Lewis Smith Lake, featuring more than 500 miles of shoreline, falls within the Bankhead National Forest's boundaries. If you want to head out of the city for a taste of wilderness, this is one region to consider. It is, however, recommended that you get a local map before hiking in the area.

"The Bankhead National Forest

is the 'crown jewel' of Alabama's wild places."

Charles Seifried
Coauthor
Alabama's Canyons

Natural Bridge
Natural Bridge, Alabama

This unique natural rock formation was created by an underground river over 200 million years ago. Creek Indians originally lived in the area and later both Confederate and Union troops used the area for camps. The structure consists of a double span sandstone bridge, and is the longest natural bridge east of the Rockies. The largest arch measures 33 feet wide, 148 feet long, and over 60 feet high. Surrounding the bridge are lush nature paths, convenient picnic areas, boulders and vegetation. Approximately 27 varieties of ferns can be spotted in the area, as well as several large Canadian hemlocks. The footpath around the arch is an easy walk taking approximately 30 minutes. The grounds also include a gift shop displaying many paintings and postcards featuring images of this scenic location.

Noccalula Falls Park
Gadsden, Alabama

Located off Lookout Mountain Parkway, the park contains something for the entire family. It features botanical gardens, an animal petting area, campgrounds, a miniature golf course, hiking trails and a pioneer homestead. That village contains numerous older log structures that have been moved to the park from sites throughout the Tennessee Valley. Most buildings contain replicas of farming equipment, furniture and artifacts from years gone by. The village and other attractions can be accessed either by walking from the office or by way of the miniature train, which the youngsters will surely enjoy. One of the park's

signature curiosities is its bronze statute of Noccalula. Legend has it that the Indian maiden was in love with a brave of her tribe and, hearing that she was to marry a wealthy suitor selected by her father, leaped to her death off the cliff into a rushing stream 90 feet below. At that same ravine, one can explore waterfalls, see rare plants and unusual rock formations, or take a two-hour hike through a historic gorge trail containing caves and numerous Indian carvings.

Hindu Cultural Center
of North Alabama
Harvest, Alabama

Many people do not realize it, but Hinduism is the oldest religion in the world. Sacred Hindu texts are the most ancient religious documents surviving today. After Christianity and Islam, Hinduism has grown to become the world's third largest religion with followers comprising more than 13 percent of the world's population. There are 1.2 million Hindus living in the United States. In the Tennessee Valley, however, there are only two Hindu temples – one in Nashville (the Sri Ganesh Temple) and the other in North Alabama. Located in Harvest, the Hindu Cultural Center of North Alabama (HCCNA) reflects Hinduism's traditions and beliefs. Its theology, which involves many types of prayers and images, is well represented at the HCCNA. Although most temples are dedicated to one deity, this temple is dedicated to over a dozen deities represented by white marble images of gods and goddesses in individual shrines. While the many types of deities might imply that Hindus worship numerous gods, such is not the case. In reality, Hindus believe there is only one God (Brahma) who is manifested through many forms. Worship services at the HCCNA are conducted throughout the day and evening in the main temple room and are attended by women draped in traditional saris and men wearing colorful robes. Activities such as yoga, meditation, and dance lessons are all conducted on a regular basis at this cultural center. The center welcomes visitors every day of the week.

"Bear no malice to others and don't expect anything in return

for the work that you do – you will be a happy person.

Let the Vedic knowledge enkindle all of us and bring 'pragna' (deep knowledge)."

Dr. Bhagabat C. Sahu
Chairman
HCCNA Board of Trustees

Huntsville Botanical Garden
Huntsville, Alabama

This botanical garden is not only a fantastic scenic location but also represents what is best about this community. Local volunteers have contributed hundreds of thousands of hours to its development. The Huntsville community organized the garden in 1981, and it has slowly grown to become one of the most scenic spots in north Alabama. Consisting of more than 110 acres, the Garden is constantly expanding and has established itself as an oasis of peace, beauty, and tranquility. It houses the nation's largest seasonal open-air butterfly house (9000 square feet), which serves as home to over 2000 butterflies. The Garden is is open to the public year round and enjoyed by more than 250,000 visitors annually. It holds numerous events, educational programs, classes, and camps throughout the year. Some of the most popular annual events and shows include: the *Butterfly House* (May to September), the *Spring Festival of Flowers* (April), the *Scarecrow Trail* (September and October), and the *Galaxy of Lights* (Thanksgiving through New Year's Eve). It also contains a gazebo, an immensely popular 2-acre children's playground, gift store, café, small railway, scenic drive, nature trails, and a variety of flower and herb gardens. All of this contributes to feelings of relaxation for all who visit. The Garden's slogan, "Something is always growing on," certainly holds true for this lush getaway.

Stevenson Railroad Depot
Stevenson, Alabama

Located in the heart of downtown Stevenson, this museum and hotel preserves an important part of railroading history through the display of hundreds of artifacts reflecting times gone by. American Indian culture, pioneer life, and Civil War events are also covered. Listed in the National Register of Historic Places, the depot was rebuilt in 1872 after a fire destroyed it years earlier. The depot adjoins the Stevenson Hotel, which was also built in 1872. Both historic structures still play vital roles in Stevenson's community and are the scene of the annual Stevenson Depot Days celebration held each June to celebrate the city's rich past.

Sand Mountain Stockyard
Kilpatrick, Alabama

City slickers, listen up! A trip to the Sand Mountain Stockyard in DeKalb County on a Saturday or Wednesday will provide an entertaining, educational look into the business of buying and selling livestock. Attendees bid on bulls, cattle, calves, horses, goats, and donkeys. The people attending these sales sit in an old-fashioned theater-type auditorium and watch the livestock parade by. While the patrons are generally dressed in flannels and jeans, and the auctions are casual and laid back, this is definitely big business. On its busiest week, this stockyard, in operation since 1972, pulls in gross sales of up to $1.2 million. Gentlemen, start your bidding!

"A horse and a big hat don't make you a cowboy.

Anybody who owns or sells or trades cattle is a cowboy."

Jon Williams
Co-owner
Sand Mountain Stockyard

Walls of Jericho
Hytop, Alabama

In the 1880s, a traveling minister made his way down into this rock-walled basin, and named the area after the site of an epic battle described in the Bible's book of Joshua. After a rather strenuous downward hike, visitors today still find themselves dwarfed by the 200-foot-tall sheer cliff walls. The seven mile round-trip journey is not to be taken lightly – good shoes and extra water are highly recommended. The natural rock formations awaiting hikers are partially obscured by foliage during warmer months, but with water to take a dip, areas to picnic, and well-marked trails, this curiosity on the Alabama/Tennessee border is an enjoyable journey regardless of what time of year you hike it.

Unclaimed Baggage Center
Scottsboro, Alabama

Turtleneck sweaters. DVD players. Diamond earrings. A slightly weathered *Three Amigos* videotape. Scottsboro's most unique shopping experience serves as home to thousands upon thousands of miscellaneous goods that were, in one way or another, lost in airline transit. Less than one percent of our nation's checked baggage ends up in this one-of-a-kind store, but what an eclectic assortment of goods it is. Since its inception in 1970, Unclaimed Baggage Center has received everything from shrunken human heads to rare violins. One lucky customer purchased a $60 painting, to later have it appraised at more than $15,000! Unclaimed Baggage Center features an impressively stocked jewelry counter, a sporting goods section, an electronics area, a clothing section, and much more. There is also, not surprisingly, a decent selection of luggage for sale!

"Some people have some really odd stuff.

You'd be amazed!"

Cindi Lewis
Shopaholic
Huntsville, Alabama

Rosenbaum House
Florence, Alabama

America's most acclaimed architect, Frank Lloyd Wright, designed only one house in the state of Alabama. The Rosenbaum House was commissioned by Stanley and Mildred Rosenbaum, and was built in 1939. The house is constructed of cypress, glass, and brick, and has been called one of the finest, purest examples of Wright's Usonian design. Ten years after its original completion, the Rosenbaums commissioned Wright to return and build an addition to the house. They lived in the house until 1999. Today, informative tours of the meticulously restored house are available for visitors. A guided walk-through gives you insight into Wright's philosophies, as well as his colorful and often stubborn personality. The house also showcases furnishings of Wright's design. A second Frank Lloyd Wright design, the Seamour Shavin House, can be found a few hours to the east in Chattanooga.

"A great architect is not made by way of a brain nearly so much as he is made by way of a cultivated, enriched heart."

Frank Lloyd Wright

CHAPTER VII:
Tennessee Festivals and Events Within the Valley
From Brewing Styles to Monkey Trials

In addition to the year-round attractions within the state of Tennessee, Valley inhabitants and visitors have a plentiful supply of seasonal events to entertain them on the weekends. Some featured festivals, like Chattanooga's Riverbend, are quite large and established. Others, like the Sorghum Squeeze Festival in Halls Mill, are relatively small, albeit highly rewarding. The majority of the featured events in the next two chapters are either free, request donations upon entry, or require entry fees of only a few dollars. The large-scale music festivals often cost more. As you would expect, the majority of festivals take place in the warmer months. But rest assured this book showcases some winter events as well. Tennessee is host to some pretty colorful happenings throughout the year. For nature lovers, springtime kicks off with the Nashville Lawn and Garden Show, and summer brings with it a treat for history buffs in the way of Dayton's passionate reenactment of the world-famous Scopes Monkey Trial. If history is not your thing, perhaps when fall rolls around the Southern Brewer's Festival is a bit more suited to your pallet. And with winter comes a healthy dose of lights, hot chocolate, and even the occasional horse-drawn buggy ride.

"Middle and Southeast Tennesseans celebrate their heritage, beauty, tradition and unique communities through a variety of wonderful festivals held each year. Throughout this entire area, you'll find an abundance of these distinctive festivals that welcome you to experience the local flavor and traditions unique to each community."

Kellye Murphy
Marketing Director
Williamson County Convention & Visitors Bureau

BRYAN
-IS A-
WINDBAG

Tennessee Arts and Crafts Association Spring Fair
Nashville, Tennessee

This arts and crafts fair has to be one of the neatest events the Tennessee Valley has to offer. With literally hundreds of guilded artists displaying and selling their creations, the turnout for this event is in the thousands. Held in grassy Centennial Park, it is also a great event for pet owners. You will see almost as many different breeds of dogs as you will artwork! Artists come from all over the state to compete and exhibit here, and the variety of artwork is both visually stunning as well as remarkably well-priced. Regardless of your artistic tastes – whether you like pottery, photography, wood, metal, watercolor, leather, glass, jewelry, or something in between – you can find it here in beautiful fashion. Chances are, you will spy a handful of things you simply cannot live without, so be sure to swing by the ATM on your way. Talking to the artists also proves to be an enjoyable experience, as they are generally eager to walk potential customers through their creative processes.

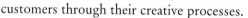

Artists, clockwise from lower left:
Robert & Donna Pitz, *Viking Cabinet Wood Sculpture w/Secret Compartments*, 2005, Maryville, Tennessee, pitzstu@aol.com
Bebo, *Mr. Blue*, 2005, Kingston Springs, Tennessee, www.bebofolkart.com
Eric Lankford, *Shark Dinner Plate*, 2004, Burns, Tennessee, www.ericlankford.com
Roy Overcast, *Assorted Tennessee Terra Cotta Pieces*, Brentwood, Tennessee, radp@bellsouth.net
Scott Wise, *Limestone Fountain*, 2004, Clarksville, Tennessee, www.scottwisesculptures.com

Railroad Rendezvous Springfest
Cookeville, Tennessee

Long before Americans zipped around this country in cars and airplanes, railroads were our primary source of long-distance transportation. Once a year in Cookeville, railroad enthusiasts flock to the Cookeville Railroad Depot to relive those days. The celebration kicks off with an authentic historic train arriving from Nashville, which then fills up and heads out for a brief round-trip excursion to Algood. This festival features mini-train rides for the kids, clowns, antique cars, and plenty of food. Model trains are also on display. The official Resonator Guitar State Championship is held during this festival, so come prepared to listen to some fantastic music. This event is enjoyable for both adults and kids alike, because trains are fun no matter how old you are!

"It's the pick for pickers and grinners! Pickers gather at the Cookeville Depot for the official Tennessee State Resonator Guitar Championship, and grinners of all ages enjoy an excursion on the historical Tennessee Central Railway Museum Train."

Ellene Duncan
Event Organizer
Railroad Rendezvous Springfest

National Cornbread Festival
South Pittsburg, Tennessee

Cornbread – a staple of Southern cuisine – is serious business in the city of South Pittsburg, Tennessee. If you think cornbread simply comes in two colors – yellow and white – and is classified as either being *regular* or *Mexican*, then you need to visit this annual festival. Upon arrival, you will be introduced to at least a dozen types of cornbread – culinary creations ranging from jalapeño-bacon cornbread to sausage cornbread and cornbread salad. Best of all, these are not heavily guarded family secrets; most recipes are provided in printed form for festival attendees. The recipes vary – ingredients can include eggs, buttermilk, regular milk, baking soda, white or yellow cornmeal, and a variety of "add-ons." Regardless of the recipe used, many contestants familiar with cooking authentic cornbread agree that a cast iron skillet and some hot grease thrown into the mixture both contribute to the process. More than likely, the cast iron skillet will have been forged at South Pittsburg's very own Lodge™ manufacturing plant, the nation's only maker of cast iron cookware. Not by coincidence, the Lodge plant is located within walking distance of the festival and is one of the sponsors of this three-day event. In addition to the cornbread tasting, numerous other activities are available throughout the weekend. Road races, arts and crafts, historic tours, food vendors, a cornbread cook-off, a cornbread-eating contest, and even bluegrass jam sessions entertain festivalgoers. You'll also find a carnival on the outskirts of the festival, and not far beyond that lies the Lodge manufacturing plant, which opens its foundry for tours during the festival.

"Perhaps no bread in the world is quite so good as Southern cornbread, and perhaps no bread in the world is quite so bad as the Northern imitation of it."

Mark Twain

Nashville Lawn and Garden Show
Nashville, Tennessee

30,000 people visiting a flower show? Believe it! At the four-day Nashville Lawn and Garden Show, you'll find such crowds from all over the South. For almost two decades, this show has provided gardening ideas, insights, and inspiration for amateur and professional gardeners alike. The show is held annually every March at the Tennessee State Fairgrounds. It showcases floral and gardening displays that take up so much space they extend throughout five different buildings. Vendors from numerous states arrange dozens of live gardens and set up hundreds of booths showcasing wildlife displays, landscaping products, and outdoor services. Speakers give lectures and horticultural organizations present topics ranging from basic gardening principles to exotic foreign styles. After spending time at this immensely popular event, you can better appreciate why gardening continues to be the most popular hobby in the United States.

"For those who dig and plant, the Nashville Lawn and Garden Show is the first indication that winter won't last forever."

**Houston Townsend
Master Gardener**

Mule Day
Columbia, Tennessee

This event, held annually in Columbia, Tennessee, honors America's favorite hybrid animal – the mule. Mule Day is actually a series of activities lasting for four days and has been a Columbia tradition since around 1840. One of the festival's major high points is the Mule Day parade, which takes place downtown. In this parade, literally thousands of mules are dressed to impress, pulling everything from wagons to funeral hearses. The parade has an old-fashioned atmosphere – you can expect to see everything from waving politicians to floats and bands. You may even see border collies coming down the street, herding sheep. Further Mule Day activities are held at nearby Maury County Park and include a mule-pulling contest, a flea market, an arts and crafts show, a knife and coin show, a mule-driving show, mule sales, square dancing, a liars' contest, and numerous food stalls. If you ever wanted to get up close and personal with a mule, here's your chance!

Shadow Valley Gospel Music Festival
Shadow Valley, Tennessee

When most people think of genuine Tennessee Valley music, they often envision the CMA Festival or Riverbend in Tennessee or Big Spring Jam in Alabama. However, you really don't need thousands of people to enjoy true Valley music. If you like gospel without the crowds or chaos, consider attending the Shadow Valley Gospel Music Festival. This festival has been held annually for more than a decade in a pleasant farm setting north of Fayetteville. For three days each July, you can enjoy true gospel music in a relaxed atmosphere reminiscent of years gone by. With an occasional donkey braying, old-fashioned funeral fans waving, and a little thigh-slapping, various groups perform to the delight of the audience spread out over the south Tennessee hillside. This is clean Christian music at its best – just bring your lawn chair and join the fun. If you wish to spend the night at the festival, RV hookups are available.

Habitat for Humanity Weekend
Alabama and Tennessee

These year-round activities take place in cities all across the Tennessee Valley. Good-hearted Samaritans aren't required to have the status of Jimmy Carter to get involved in a Habitat for Humanity project. Every weekend, both in the Tennessee Valley and around the world, volunteers perform both construction and nonconstruction activities to build homes for the needy. Since 1976, more than 200,000 homes have been built by this international organization. Habitat for Humanity provides families with the life-changing opportunity to own decent, affordable homes. This noble cause relies upon the assistance of numerous volunteers to help with duties ranging from office work and transportation to landscaping and carpentry. The homeowners must provide "sweat equity" in the building of their home. In Tennessee, there are 57 local Habitat chapters, and in Alabama, 39. If you are interested in working a Habitat weekend on a strictly volunteer basis, visit www.habitat.org for a listing of local affiliates and their work schedules. This is one feel-good outing that can enhance the lives of everyone involved.

"It's an opportunity to really live out our faith."

Doug Seay
House Leader
Habitat for Humanity of Madison County

Riverbend Festival
Chattanooga, Tennessee

"Riverbend rocks."

Marcus Lourant
Drummer

While there are many musical events in the Valley, Chattanooga's Riverbend Festival has become one of the biggest. It is now larger than both Huntsville's Big Spring Jam and Manchester's Bonnaroo. Riverbend originated in 1981, and over the years it has gradually expanded to run for nine consecutive nights. Riverbend now includes more than 100 different performing acts, sprawling across six separate stages. It is arguably the city's most beloved event, with crowds estimated in excess of 650,000 people for the entire festival. Because the festival is so spread out along the riverfront, you do not feel as crowded as you might expect at a party of this magnitude. The main arena is a unique multi-level floating stage, and is the premier landmark location of the festival. The other stages accommodate artists of all musical genres (there is also a children's stage) allowing you to track down just about any type of music you enjoy. In addition to a long string of food concessions along the river, there are numerous commercial stalls, booths, and exhibits that provide nonmusical entertainment and educational activities. Riverbend is one of the biggest, most exciting musical events in the South, and the number of families that come from near and far is a testament to the top-notch quality of this festival.

Scopes Monkey Trial Reenactment

Dayton, Tennessee

In 1925, John Scopes, a substitute biology teacher, was accused of teaching the theory of evolution and natural selection to his rural high school class. Tennessee state law prohibited teaching evolution in a public school. Scopes's actions led to a criminal proceeding featuring Clarence Darrow against William Jennings Bryan in a science-versus-religion debate that raised eyebrows across the nation. At the conclusion of the trial, Scopes was found guilty and fined $100 for his teachings. Since 1987, Dayton's Chamber of Commerce has presented this annual reenactment, which exposes the explosive issues surrounding the true origins of humankind. Performed in the same Rhea County courtroom where it all happened, the play is part of a three-day commemorative festival. Held each July, it not only relives one of history's most famous trials but also revives the arguments concerning creationism (now often referred to as "Intelligent Design") versus science-based evolution. If you are interested in revisiting historical events at their actual locations, this is one production that is sure to please. The festival also features craft booths, food, pony rides, and classic car displays. The Scopes Museum – located in the basement of the courthouse, is open to visitors throughout the festival weekend.

"In 1925, the Scopes Trial was both a publicity stunt designed to attract business and industry to Dayton and a serious effort to test the validity of the Tennessee anti-evolution statute. The festival seeks to re-create the festive atmosphere that surrounded the trial, and offer a serious, historically accurate look at one of America's most significant legal battles. The issues raised in the Scopes Trial, far beyond just the creation-evolution controversy, are as hotly debated today as they were in 1925."

Tom Davis
Festival Chairman

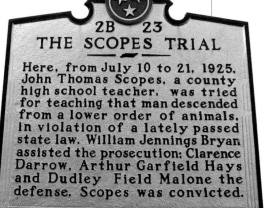

2B 23
THE SCOPES TRIAL

Here, from July 10 to 21, 1925, John Thomas Scopes, a county high school teacher, was tried for teaching that man descended from a lower order of animals, in violation of a lately passed state law. William Jennings Bryan assisted the prosecution; Clarence Darrow, Arthur Garfield Hays and Dudley Field Malone the defense. Scopes was convicted.

CMA Music Festival
Nashville, Tennessee

If you like country music, the CMA (Country Music Association) Music Festival is for you. Every year the who's who of toe-tappin', guitar-strummin', boot-wearin', chart-toppers come to Nashville to perform for fans. Daytime activities range from riverside mechanical bull riding to autograph opportunities with some of country music's biggest names. Live music entertains crowds alongside the Cumberland River during the day, and the party moves into the Coliseum, home to the NFL's Tennessee Titans, in the evening. Nightly lineups always include a healthy number of today's top country stars, and the festival has a well-deserved reputation for dropping superstar guest performers onto the stage unannounced! These nightly crowds draw well over 40,000 music lovers. A particularly noteworthy feature of the CMA Music Festival is the ever-popular photo line, which allows processions of fans to walk right up to the stage and see their favorite performers up close. During the festival, the Ryman Auditorium hosts the CMA Celebrity Up Close question and answer session, where country's stars discuss everything from their upcoming tours to their favorite candy bars. The festival organizers really do make this experience as fan-oriented as possible. Families can enjoy the Family Zone, where kids can enjoy activities ranging from face painting to magic shows. All together, this four-day festival draws more than 160,000 fans into the heart of Nashville's downtown area. Posters and t-shirts proclaim the CMA Festival to be "country music's biggest party," and that claim has certainly rung true year after year!

"The CMA Festival is a really nice oportunity to strap on your boots and catch some great country music. Lots of cowgirls, too, which is always a nice plus."

Jonathan Fowler
Festival Attendee

RC Cola and MoonPie Festival
Bell Buckle, Tennessee

"The RC Cola and MoonPie Festival is easy to find but hard to leave. It's a cross between Lake Woebegone and Saturday Night Live."

Billy Phillips
Chairman
RC Cola and MoonPie Festival

The cozy town of Bell Buckle, Tennessee, serves as host to what might be the heavyweight champion of off-beat, peculiar Southern festivals. The brainchild of three local ladies, the RC Cola and MoonPie Festival is a celebration of the Tennessee Valley's two favorite junk foods. When attending this festival, expect to see a delightful array of lighthearted, down-home entertainment, including skits, dances, clogging, "synchronized wading," and more. MoonPies (for those of you who have either been living under a rock or have just recently moved to the South) are tasty treats made of marshmallow and chocolate. They also come in other varieties, including vanilla, banana, and lemon. For MoonPie connoisseurs, this festival is a pretty good place to hunt down those lesser-known, more elusive flavors! But don't concern yourself with whether or not there will be a healthy sampling of other culinary options – there are plenty of booths serving everything from Tennessee smoked barbeque to Philly cheesesteaks. The recommended dessert and beverage of choice, however, should be obvious!

Tennessee Walking Horse National Celebration
Shelbyville, Tennessee

As the title indicates, the Tennessee Walking Horse National Celebration is just that – a true celebration that features a multitude of activities for the entire family. Held annually in Shelbyville, Tennessee, this celebration lasts 11 days and nights prior to Labor Day. The event originated in 1939 and has steadily grown throughout the years. Currently, approximately a quarter of a million people visit the beautiful 105-acre complex every year. The area features very attractive walking grounds, a 30,000-seat outdoor stadium, a covered warm-up ring, and a large indoor arena, which

holds 4,500 people. The grounds also contain a Celebration Piazza, a Hall of Fame, the Owners' Wall, and a Celebration Trade Fair. During the course of the festival, there are numerous activities available for just about everyone, including a stable decorating contest, a barbeque cook-off, a dog show, and a karaoke contest. Old and young riders alike can participate in numerous events during this celebration. More than 2,000 horses and owners compete for the numerous ribbons, prizes, and trophies given out during this time. On the last night, the judges select the World Grand Champion Tennessee Walking Horse. And with competition at this level, you can bet this horse will be one impressive animal.

Bonnaroo
Manchester, Tennessee

Although this festival is a relative newcomer to the Tennessee Valley, Bonnaroo certainly has a huge following of fans. About 100,000 people attend each year, along with tents, sleeping bags, and tie-dye t-shirts. It is Tennessee's version of Woodstock, with all of the highs and lows therein. One thing is a sure-fire bet at Bonnaroo – excellent music. Big name performers often get the opportunity to join one another on stage, and the performances that result are often extraordinary. The Dave Matthews Band, The Black Crowes, Widespread Panic, and the Allman Brothers are examples of featured guests from previous years. Regardless of weather conditions, once the bands take the stage, the fields are filled to capacity with ecstatic crowds.

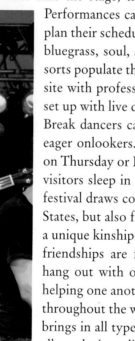

Performances carry on late into the night, and concertgoers carefully plan their schedules around who takes which stage at what time. Rock, bluegrass, soul, and even rap music is represented. Attractions of all sorts populate the grounds. Turntables for aspiring amateur DJs are on site with professionals lending instruction. Glass-blowing booths are set up with live demonstrations, often with pipes and trinkets for sale. Break dancers can be seen spinning on their heads before crowds of eager onlookers. The vast majority of Bonnaroo ticketholders arrive on Thursday or Friday, and stay throughout the entire weekend. Most visitors sleep in tents, which they pitch right next to their cars. This festival draws concertgoers from not only every corner of the United States, but also from countries around the world. You will discover a unique kinship between the majority of Bonnaroo guests. Instant friendships are formed as people discuss musical preferences and hang out with one another. Complete strangers can often be seen helping one another pitch tents, and a feeling of camaraderie prevails throughout the weekend. As far as people-watching goes, this festival brings in all types! Dredlocks, afros, tattoos, and body piercings are all on glorious display. Young college partiers turn out for this event, as do original flower children of the 1960s – and plenty of folks in between. This is not an event for children, but everyone who attends will certainly be feeling young at heart in no time.

Jack Daniel's World Championship Invitational Barbecue
Lynchburg, Tennessee

According to the Southeast Tourism Society, this event, held each October in Lynchburg, Tennessee, is consistently one of the *Top 20 Events* in the southeastern United States. In addition to the delicious food served, the reason for such popularity lies in the diversity of the competition. Sponsored by the Kansas City Barbeque Society, the festival is an international event drawing teams from both the United States and around the world. Dozens of teams travel from all over the country to attend. Numerous international teams, proudly displaying their national flags, also compete for ribbons, trophies, and cash. The two-day event starts with a parade of the contestants marching from Wiseman Park to Lynchburg Square, and then to the nearby visitor center. The competition – known as "The Jack" – is unusual in that it is by invitation only, and all U.S. teams must be "grand champions" within the current barbeque season. Some teams, initially invited as state "automatics" under the current rules, later enter "state draws," where competitors are further selected by a type of lottery system. A large team of barbeque experts judge each entry on a point system for appearance, taste, and tenderness. Cooking categories include sauces, whole hog, chicken, pork ribs, pork shoulders/butts, beef brisket, and desserts. To be eligible for "Grand Champion," a team must submit entries in four of the five meat categories. While a few of the teams operate concession stands and sell barbeque to the public, the emphasis is on the competition itself. In addition to the competition, there are a variety of events for the entire family. Unique games found at the Invitational include the Country Dog Contest, Ladies Rolling Pin Toss, Butt Bowling, and the Barrel Bung Toss. There is also a "Shade Tree Cook-off" for barbeque amateurs with their pickup trucks and Weber grills. You can also experience clogging on the town square, numerous craft tents, and entertainment by the Jack Daniel's Original Silver Cornet Band, which plays "old-timey" music for festivalgoers throughout the final day.

"The Jack Daniel's World Championship Invitational Barbecue is to barbeque contests as the Masters Tournament is to golf. It's the best of the best and by invitation only. To qualify, you have to first be a grand champion … and then you have to be lucky."

James Britt
Roadside Grill Cooking Team
Two-Time First Place Winner, Whole Hog Competition

The Battle of Franklin
Civil War Reenactment
Spring Hill, Tennessee

On November 29, 1864, General John Bell Hood's Army of Tennessee crossed the Duck River and converged on Spring Hill – the first step in his attempt to take control of Nashville. What followed was the Battle of Spring Hill, followed by the Battle of Franklin, and then the Battle of Nashville. For three consecutive days each fall, the events that transpired here are commemorated in grand fashion. Approximately 10,000 reenactors and more than 50,000 spectators come out to relive those history-shaping events. In addition to the battle reenactments themselves, other attractions include live period music, speakers, equipment displays, and historical personalities of all varieties. Reenactors are generally quite eager to strike up conversations in character and answer any questions you may throw their way. Tents are set up for embalmers, cooks, gunsmiths, and the like. The battles are nothing short of spectacular, with loads of troop movements, scores of galloping horses (especially popular with the kids), and plenty of thundering cannon fire. Civil War reenactments rarely get much bigger or better than this one!

"The Battle of Franklin was a hard fought and bloody combat,

… a turning point in a decisive campaign … the beginning of the end."

General Jacob D. Cox
(USA) Commander, 23rd Corps

The Lincoln County Fair

Fayetteville, Tennessee

For more than 100 years, the Lincoln County Fair has entertained people of the Tennessee Valley in a very special way. Unlike a typical festival where the emphasis is on commercial food and musical entertainment, this event is reminiscent of days gone by. For nine days and nights, the fair features numerous down-home activities both young and old will enjoy. 4-H members and local students compete in numerous events. Some of the South's best gardeners, cooks, and artists have stalls set up to display their wares. If you like animals, the fair showcases market hogs, sheep, dairy goats, cattle and rabbit shows, pony and mule races, and livestock exhibits. Cooking and produce contests, beauty contests, and carnival rides are just a few of the many activities the fair regularly sponsors. The fair also features nationally known and regional musical acts on Saturday nights for the whole family. And don't forget the famous harness races! The Lincoln County Fair is the last remaining haven in the state for this equine sport. Day and nighttime races are held at a fast half-mile track where you can sit in a modern grand-stand to view this exciting event. Officially a nonprofit organization, the Lincoln County Fair represents a pleasant journey into childhood memories that is annually enjoyed by more than 100,000 people.

"In addition to sponsoring the only harness racing in Tennessee, the Lincoln County Fair represents one full week of fun for the entire family."

Cindy Harwell
Chairperson
Harness Racing Event

Southern Brewer's Festival
Chattanooga, Tennessee

Benjamin Franklin once made the statement, "Beer is proof that God loves us and wants us to be happy." If this is the case, then visitors to the Southern Brewer's Festival must be among the happiest, most well-loved people in the region. With dozens of award-winning beers from microbreweries around the country, this celebration donates its proceeds to the Make-A-Wish Foundation of East Tennessee. Selections range from various pale ales to blueberry-flavored beer (yes, blueberry!). Held on the banks of the Tennessee River, this jovial event is a great excuse to loosen your belt and put that low-carb diet on hold. Attendees are each issued a mug at the entrance, and round, wooden "beer tokens" are purchased and exchanged for refills. Food and live music are also in healthy supply.

"If you can't have fun at the beer festival, it is your own damn fault!"

**Neve Weinberger
Beer Lover**

Sorghum Squeeze Festival
Halls Mill, Tennessee

Obscure, small, and yet bursting with old-time country culture, the Sorghum Squeeze Festival is one of the region's more unique and colorful additions to its list of autumn activities. Located a short drive from Shelbyville in the shadow of an old farmhouse in Halls Mill, this annual celebration provides an enjoyable lesson on what it takes to make sorghum. Sorghum, for those wondering what the heck it is in the first place, is a tall cane crop. Farmers cut down, crush, and drain the stalks, then boil and filter the extracted liquid to separate out a sweet syrup. The final product is then bottled or generously drizzled over hot biscuits, pancakes, and the like. At the festival, you can witness the entire age-old process – from stalk to syrup – and then enjoy the sweet rewards at nearby picnic tables. You can also watch the cane-splitting operation (powered by a harnessed mule), enjoy the "old-timey" dancers in their period costumes, or find out for yourself what a house built in the 1700s looks like.

Goats, Music and More Festival
Lewisburg, Tennessee

This appropriately named festival proudly features both the Southern Tennessee Boer Goat Show and the World Championship Fainting Goat Show. Yes, fainting goats. Since the 1880s, Marshall County has been home to an extended family of easily rattled, stiff-legged goats, which upon being surprised or frightened, tense up and tip over. This apparent fainting is actually caused by a neuromuscular condition called myotonia, but rest assured, this condition does not harm the goats. The Boer goat is a fairly large animal, weighing more than 200 pounds and colored with reddish-brown and white fur. This festival allows for visitors and competitors alike to meet the who's who in the world of championship goating, along with some other fairly 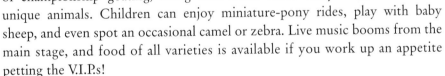 unique animals. Children can enjoy miniature-pony rides, play with baby sheep, and even spot an occasional camel or zebra. Live music booms from the main stage, and food of all varieties is available if you work up an appetite petting the V.I.P.s!

Tennessee Valley Oktoberfests
Tennessee and Alabama

Dust off the accordions and tap the beer kegs! From Crossville to Cullman, come autumn, almost every major city within the Tennessee Valley throws an Oktoberfest of some variation to welcome in the changing of the leaves. The origins of this festival can be traced back to the German city of Munich, where almost two centuries ago King Ludwig of Bavaria threw a heck of a party to celebrate his wedding to Princess Therese of Saxony-Hildburghausen. Ludwig invited *every resident* in the city, and ultimately more than 40,000 partiers got in on the festivities. Now granted, our local Valley Oktoberfests don't generally bring in crowds of that magnitude. They do, however, offer you ample opportunity to chow down on traditional German cuisine, including schnitzel, kasseler rippchen, bratwursts, and knackwursts. Partiers eat, drink, and dance the night away to the music of the Oompah bands. You are not required to don the traditional German attire, but Oktoberfest purists will certainly arrive in lederhosen, with their socks pulled up above the calf! German beer is as much a staple at an Oktoberfest as German food, so get out your favorite stein and designate a driver – unless, of course, the Oktoberfest is held in a dry county! There are too many Oktoberfests in the Tennessee Valley to list, but if you start searching the Internet and scanning the newspapers in late September, chances are you will find one or two in your area with little difficulty. Many of the Valley's Oktoberfests are kid-friendly, offering activity areas for children while parents enjoy grown-up festivities.

"'Ein Prosit, ein Prosit, der
Gemuetlichkeit' ... hoert man
immer wieder in Muenchen auf
dem Oktoberfest seit 1810. Es ist
ein freudiger Anlass zum Feiern
und Zusammen sein."

Margaret Hays
Huntsville, Alabama

Tennessee History Festival
Nashville, Tennessee

Few history lessons are as compelling and engaging as those that come from fully-costumed, well-informed reenactors. The Tennessee History Festival is a relatively new event to the region, but due to the dedication of its players, it offers a fantastic experience. As you explore the area, you'll encounter such historical figures as Andrew Jackson and Frederick Douglas. You will often overhear other festivalgoers asking questions such as, "And who are you?" and "When did you live?" Many of the reenactors have set up supporting displays, such as a Civil War-era field surgeon's tent, or a World War II operations center. Several displays showcase actual, historical artifacts, while others use replicas. Hundreds of local schoolchildren attend a staged production on the first day of the festival, where they receive a thorough history lesson from Tennessee's very own David Crockett.

Pumpkin Harvest Festival

Waynesboro, Tennessee

For more than a decade, Waynesboro residents have grabbed their gloves and scarves, headed downtown, and celebrated autumn with the Pumpkin Harvest Festival. The festival's biggest selling points are its auto show (featuring motorcycles and cars) and parade. The parade features a raucous line of locals who arrive via all manner of transportation methods. A few of the more colorful parade additions include riders on horseback, fire engines with flashing lights, and youngsters enthusiastically tossing handfuls of candy to onlookers. This is a relatively small festival, but it comes with a healthy dose of barbeque, local vendors, live music, and of course, pumpkins!

Tennessee Titans Pro-Football Games
Nashville, Tennessee

No travels to fall or winter weekend events within the Valley could be complete without a trip to Nashville's Coliseum. This is home to the area's largest professional sports team – the Tennessee Titans. If you are planning on going, however, order your tickets the previous summer – long before the season starts – or be prepared to pay

inflated scalper prices at the stadium the day of the game. Win, lose, or draw, the Titans' football games are so popular that for years the home games have been sold out at the very beginning of the season. With colorful halftime shows, fanatic supporters, beer and soda vendors, energetic cheerleaders, and, of course, the Tennessee Titans themselves, this Nashville experience is a full-on blitz of excitement.

Trees of Christmas
Manchester, Tennessee

Who better to decorate a room full of Christmas trees than the members of a garden club? For the past 29 years, a Manchester-area group – the Dig 'n' Dream Garden Club – has hosted the Trees of Christmas, a collection of theme-based creations for visitors to enjoy. This collection of symbolic creations has often featured up to 20 different decorated trees, meticulously pieced together by diligent club members in their spare time. Past themes have ranged from famous songs and well-known books to different countries – and most recently – colorful U.S. cities. As a daytime activity, garden club members offer group book readings to local schoolchildren. Each December, between 1,500 and 2,000 attendees stop by this small but unique winter event.

A Dickens of a Christmas
Franklin, Tennessee

Downtown Franklin is an attractive little city to begin with. Throw in some carriage rides, a little hot chocolate, and some impressively costumed characters from *A Christmas Carol* and it becomes a place that would make even that old curmudgeon Ebenezer Scrooge stifle his humbugs! This unique winter event, held every December, certainly justifies braving the elements to enjoy streetside carolers, 19th-century food, horses, and the occasional opportunity to converse with the Ghosts of Christmas Past, Present, and Future. Approximately 60 different vendors are set up in tents, so be sure to bring along some spending cash.

"When you hear the clatter of horses' hooves, smell the roasted chestnuts, and see the whole town in costume, it isn't difficult to imagine Franklin as a 19th-century English village."

Nancy Williams
Main Street Director
Downtown Franklin Association

"Bundle up, hold hands, and immerse yourself in the magical, natural beauty of the season."

Karen Baker
Marketing Director
See Rock City

Rock City's
Enchanted Garden of Lights
Chattanooga, Tennessee

As if Lookout Mountain wasn't cool enough already. Every winter, Santa's elves use whatever energies they have left to sprinkle some Christmas magic around Rock City. Over a quarter of a million lights give this naturally scenic oddity a completely different look. From Nativity scenes to elf statues, yuletide curiosities pepper the walk and make for fun surprises at every turn. The path winds and snakes its way through Rock City's peculiar natural formations, and as you traverse the walkway, scenes range from the petite to the extravagant. Discover more than 25 Christmas scenes at this award-winning spectacle, complete with hot chocolate, gingerbread cookies, and the usual stunning views of Chattanooga. Because much of the route is exposed to the elements, be sure to bundle up. The Garden plugs in around mid-November, and you have until New Year's to enjoy its sights.

Gaylord Opryland at Christmastime
Nashville, Tennessee

You don't have to stay at the Gaylord Opryland Resort and Convention Center to enjoy the Christmas celebrations at this magnificent resort. A drive around the resort reveals a multitude of outdoor decorations with acres of white Christmas lights. Once inside, browse and shop at numerous stores before strolling through nine acres of lush indoor gardens and pathways. Opryland also features a laser-light and fountain show, a 44-foot waterfall, and tours aboard the Delta Flatboat – right inside the hotel. This world-famous resort houses more than 2,900 rooms, plus 200 suites. With a multitude of restaurants ranging from an Irish pub to a sushi bar to a steakhouse, you can certainly find something on Opryland's menu to satisfy your appetite. If you wish to leave Opryland's main facilities, consider visiting the nearby General Jackson Showboat. The showboat features festive holiday shows throughout the Christmas season.

*"It just seems magical.
Like you simply
stepped into a different
world for a while."*

**Abheek Reddy
Opryland Guest**

*"Our yearly preparation for the Christmas season starts in July and is completed
by mid-November. We have 37 people working on our outside decorations
nonstop. The external lights alone consist of over 2,000,000 light bulbs.
But anyone who has seen it knows that it's worth it."*

Opryland Representative

Old-Fashioned Rodeos

Tennessee and Alabama

When most people think of a rodeo, they usually envision an event held somewhere out West. Rodeos, however, are held throughout the country with many different styles and formats. In the Valley, rodeos often take place in late winter or early spring. One of the most popular organizations to produce

such shows is the Longhorn World Championship Rodeo. This association usually sponsors events where contestants pay their entry fees in hopes of trophies, recognition, and cash. Typical events at a rodeo include bareback bronc riding, calf roping, bull riding, cowgirl barrel racing, saddle bronc riding, steer wrestling, and the Pony Express (gymnastics on horseback). Anyone who has ever witnessed a 2,000-pound raging Brahma bull charge after a rider, or watched a rodeo clown scramble to protect a cowboy, knows that this is one visceral sport that generates plenty of adrenaline for participants and spectators alike.

Tennessee State Fairgrounds December Flea Market

Nashville, Tennessee

Every second weekend of every month, visitors travel from far and wide to shop at the Tennessee State Fairgrounds. Vendors from 30 states set up booths for business. During the second weekend of December, however, the fair provides an especially rewarding shopping experience. The holiday season brings forth more vendors, more customers, and more deals. Children can visit with Santa while adults wander for hours browsing for jewelry, clothes, tools, crafts, and hundreds of thousands of other items. Although parking costs a few dollars, the fair itself is free to all and is a great opportunity to stock up on gifts, essentials, and curiosities.

"This is the biggest fair I know of.

I am buying almost all of my Christmas stuff here."

Mindy Kimball
Fair Visitor

A Christmas Tour by Land or Water
Throughout the Valley

Deck the halls with boughs of holly! In and around the holiday season, nearly every community in the Tennessee Valley sponsors some sort of local scenic tour. These can range from parades of homes where you can walk or drive through neighborhoods to horse-drawn carriage rides sponsored by historical foundations and tourism boards. Beautiful scenes abound, both at the individually decked-out homes and in the streets themselves. Block after block of sidewalks often sparkle with elegant luminaries. And don't limit your tours strictly to the local neighborhoods. Some of the South's most attractive antebellum homes located in Chattanooga, Nashville, and other Civil War-era cities are immaculately decorated for the occasion. From log cabin Christmas tours such as the one in Elkton, Tennessee, to the numerous parades of boats and boating regattas on the Tennessee River, residents in this part of the country spare no effort in decorating for the holiday season.

CHAPTER VIII:
Alabama Festivals
and Events Within the Valley
From Hot Air Balloons to Bluegrass Tunes

In the riverside city of Decatur, a handful of crazy Alabamians kick off the first day of each new year by taking an exhilarating New Year's plunge into the Tennessee River. That pretty much sets the tone for Alabama's fun approach to festivals! Some really entertaining events take place in north Alabama, such as eagle-watching excursions in Guntersville, a renaissance faire in Florence, and a unique cemetery stroll held in Huntsville. Food festivals are in good supply as well, with Alabama celebrating the usual foods, like barbeque and catfish, and the unique, like the Poke Weed. Much like its neighbor to the north, Alabama plays host to Civil War reenactments, music festivals, and art festivals. If you are in search of a weekend festival, chances are you can find one to your liking in north Alabama.

"North Alabama is one of the true garden spots of the earth.
It is a remarkable setting for scores of outdoor festivals that range from
music and mountain crafts to barbeque and fish fries."

Lee Sentell
Alabama State Tourism Director

Maple Hill Cemetery Stroll
Huntsville, Alabama

Although there are literally hundreds of events throughout the Valley, few provide colorful perspectives into local history like the annual stroll through Maple Hill Cemetery in Huntsville. Sponsored by the Huntsville Pilgrimage Association, Maple Hill Cemetery, established in 1818, is full of history written on headstones, mausoleums, and monuments. More than 80 costumed characters from history are represented by local residents who discuss the characters' lives at the tombstones in one of the most historic and attractive cemeteries in the Valley. These characters include five Alabama governors, and soldiers of the Revolutionary, 1812, Spanish-American, and Civil wars. A host of local "personalities," including ghosts, a madam, and a famous local cow, are also available for interviews! Costumed musical groups, complete with musical instruments of the period, play a variety of music throughout the cemetery. Maple Hill Cemetery is the oldest and largest cemetery in the state of Alabama. The cemetery has 97 acres and is the  final resting place to more than 85,000 people. As you enter the cemetery, you will be given a map denoting the locations of the characters, the time frames involved, and the name of the residents portraying the historical individuals and groups. This "voice from Huntsville's past" is certainly a learning experience for all. Throughout the last several years, approximately 5,000 people have annually attended this educational, fun, and free activity.

Hot Air Balloon Classic
Decatur, Alabama

This huge gathering is not only one of Alabama's most popular events but arguably one of the most beautiful spectator sports in the Tennessee Valley. The Classic involves more than 60 pilots from 20 states and, weather permitting, results in a sky filled with a rainbow of seven-story balloons of every shape and color. The early-morning activities are unique in that they allow for a crowd of approximately 50,000 to mingle with pilots. Visitors and pilots chitchat while the balloons are inflated for the competition. During the three-day festival, there is a "keygrab" competition, where balloonists attempt to capture a key mounted on a tall pole. Festivities also include a "balloon glow" at sunset, which is a breathtaking sight to behold! Other festival attractions include a fireworks extravaganza, an antique tractor and classic car show, an international food court, arts and crafts booths, stage entertainment, and events for children. The Classic is held every Memorial Day weekend on the grounds of Point Mallard Park, a municipal recreation complex located in Decatur.

"Flying is more than a feeling, it's a freedom.

You really can't explain it until you have experienced it."

Cindi Jacob
Pilot, Ms. Independence
Baton Rouge, Louisiana

The Balloonist's Prayer

The winds have welcomed you with softness
The sun has blessed you with his warm hands
You have flown so high and so well
That God joined you in your laughter
And he has set you gently back again
Into the loving arms of Mother Earth.

Panoply
Huntsville, Alabama

Panoply, Huntsville's annual arts festival, is held downtown in scenic Big Spring Park at the end of April. This festival caters to the young at heart, and to all those who have an appreciation for aesthetics. Held in Huntsville for more than two decades, Panoply is supported by more than 2,000 volunteers and often draws 90,000 people during its three-day period. It is one of the largest festivals in north Alabama. Unlike most festivals of this size, Panoply is, for the most part, dedicated to children. The emphasis of the many sponsors is not only to entertain the children, but also to provide unique experiences of hands-on art. The entertainment is continuous, with local and regional entertainers performing theatrical works, dances, and songs on five different arena stages. Recent additions to Panoply include the Alabama State Fiddling Championship and a large cultural exhibit known as the *Global Village*. Numerous art tents are set up to display different types of paintings, illustrations, and other various creations by schoolchildren from throughout the region. Kids' creations are submitted for competition, and awards are given out accordingly. You can also find woodworking, pottery, sculptures, jewelry, and photography at Panoply. The festival features a variety of fun and free activities, which are available for the kids throughout the day, including face painting and various craft projects they can take home with them. Children ages 12 and under are admitted to Panoply free of charge.

"Panoply is a good place to see lots of different art styles. Sometimes artists are there to tell you how they did stuff. And that's cool too."

Darnell Winters
Future Comic Book Artist

Poke Salat Festival
Arab, Alabama

Arab, Alabama, located approximately 18 miles south of Huntsville, is the home of the one and only annual Poke Salat Festival. Poke salat is made from pokeweed and is commonly known as "the poor man's greens." It is a wild plant found throughout the area. Other names (and spellings) for this plant are poke sallat, poke salad, poke berries, poke root, scote, pigeonberry, and inkweed, to name a few. Be sure to only eat the young shoots after they have been boiled twice – the rest of the plant, including older leaves, is toxic. It is important to note that local folklore claims that Poke salat can be used at a new moon to break hexes! On the first night of the festival (a Friday) the activities kick off with a concert at the local high school. On Saturday the festival features a street fair, children's activities, arts and crafts, antique cars, and (naturally) a Poke salat cookoff. All of this is followed by a free, fun-filled street dance later that evening.

The Lure of the River
Throughout the Valley

"Fishing is much more than fish. It is the great occasion when we may return to the fine simplicity of our forefathers."
Herbert Hoover

Some folks living in the Tennessee Valley have no interest in attending the region's unique festivals and attractions. Others totally ignore the historically significant locations that abound within a day's drive. For many, the Valley means one thing only – the Tennessee River. And that, in turn, means fishing. From TVA's Fort Loudon Dam in eastern Tennessee to the Kentucky Dam toward the end of the river, the current 650-mile navigation channel of the Tennessee River provides an unending playground for fishermen throughout the South. Bass, perch, spots, bream, blues, catfish, and crappie are just a few of the many species found in the area. And we're not talking small fish. Local fishermen have caught catfish weighing more than 80 pounds in the areas below the many dams throughout the region. You will need a state fishing license to pursue this activity, but it is well worth it. Amateur tournaments, fishing rodeos, and family outings each provide a perfect venue for enjoying the great outdoors along the water. Taking your family to picnic and fish along the river or a TVA reservoir, or simply "drowning worms" for an hour or two in a backwater stream is pure enjoyment for all involved!

Pro Fishing Tournaments
From Guntersville to Pickwick and Beyond

And then there are the professional tournaments – which can also be referred to as NASCAR on the water. These take place in both Alabama and Tennessee. Anyone who thinks this is a relaxing, relatively inexpensive, low-intensity sport has obviously never been exposed to one of these contests. Sponsored by such national organizations as B.A.S.S. and Wal-Mart FLW Tours, these tournaments are a big money sport, with purses often exceeding a million dollars for a weekend event. Entry fees for pros can be in the thousands of dollars, and co-anglers often pay several hundred dollars to participate. The tournaments are conducted throughout the year and are well advertised, both nationally and within the region. The professional anglers on these circuits generally have top-of-the-line bass boats, most with identical outboard motors. Just like NASCAR, all equipment used must meet strict specifications established by tournament sponsors. Also similar to NASCAR, spectators at the events will witness participants traveling at top speed. The pros spend as much time fishing as they can and often race back to the docks at the last second to meet their deadlines. International media coverage and world-class outdoor programs often accompany these tournaments, where the world's top bass anglers compete against one another in timed events lasting several days. Spectators regularly line up to witness the "flights" leaving the docks early in the morning and return in the afternoons for the tournament weigh-ins. The weigh-ins are strictly regulated and are usually held in huge tents with hundreds of spectators monitoring large computer screens which display the results and the daily rankings of the participants. A pro tournament provides excitement galore for the novice and outdoorsman alike. And yes, sometimes even the pros return empty-handed!

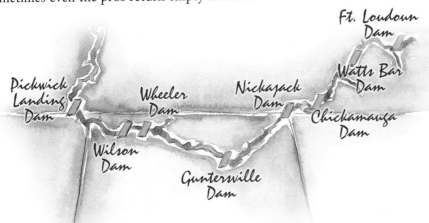

"Touring the circuit on a yearly basis is fun. You meet a lot of interesting people, it's exciting, and sometimes very rewarding. Even if it has cost me a couple marriages."

Pro-angler Who Prefers to Remain Anonymous

Moontown Air Show

Moontown, Alabama

Airplane lovers, helicopter fans, and ultralight hobbyists stroll the grassy Moontown airfield (northeast of Huntsville) for one weekend every April to check out what their fellow aviators are flying. During these three days, you can examine everything from bulky old biplanes to petite new lightweights. Brilliantly colored aircraft constantly swoop in and jet out, while kids and adults alike snack on goodies and talk shop. Every pilot has a story to tell, and many wide-eyed aces-to-be can be seen listening attentively, hoping for a chance to go up into the clouds.

"You see everything from Russian military airplanes to homebuilts to ultralights,

and you can take a ride in a classic barnstormer-era biplane.

The food is great and the setting is beautiful. I recommend it highly."

Joe Lofton
Private Pilot

Tim's Cajun Kitchen Crawfish Festival
Huntsville, Alabama

Would you believe that there's a place where folks devour more than 7,000 pounds of crawfish in just seven hours? Believe it or not, that's what they do at Tim's Cajun Kitchen Crawfish Festival held annually at Huntsville's Von Braun Center. In addition to crawfish, you can order up other tasty Creole dishes such as étouffée, boudin, alligator, and jambalaya. In keeping with the Cajun atmosphere, dancers swing to a variety of music ranging from zydeco to country and western. If you have never heard a zydeco band – usually featuring washboards and other unique musical instruments – it is a high-energy, fun-filled experience! And even if you don't care for the Louisiana musical scene, you should at least swing by with an appetite and try the unique cuisine served at this distinctive event.

SCOOP & SERVE
BOUDIN (1 STICK) — 2.00
RED BEANS & RICE — 6.00
GUMBO — 6.00
JAMBALAYA — 6.00
CRAWFISH ETOUFEE 6.00

The Chicken and Egg Festival
Moulton, Alabama

If you want an answer to the age-old question of which came first, the chicken or the egg, then this has got the be the best place on earth to ask. Two full days are dedicated entirely to Moulton's love of poultry. As far as chicken-and-egg festivities go, if you can imagine it, they have got it. Sponsors hold chicken-cooking contests, an egg toss, chicken-eating competitions, chicken-clucking contests, and even boiled egg-eating contests. This event offers plenty of food to eat (of course), plenty of music to listen to, and plenty of activities to occupy the youngsters. This is a fairly new addition to the Tennessee Valley's list of unusual annual festivals, but it is a great excuse to get some sunshine and protein in your diet!

Parent/Child Weekend at U.S. Space Camp
Huntsville, Alabama

Try something out of this world! Since 1982, U.S. Space Camp has provided both young-sters and adults with an overview of space exploration and realistic mission simulations. Throughout the year, Space Camp offers a variety of educational activities. In addition to week-long and multi-week programs, Space Camp offers quick parent/child weekends where families can enjoy the challenges of space travel simulations. The core of Space Camp, modeled after NASA's astronaut-training facility at Houston's Lyndon B. Johnson Space Center, features hands-on programs that give its students a firsthand opportunity to experience shuttle launches, space missions, and walks on the moon. Space Camp is designed to encourage young people to pursue careers in aerospace, science, math, and other related fields. This camp, as well as the Parent/Child Aviation Challenge, offers many group programs of various lengths. These types of programs provide whole-some, educational, bonding experiences for family members. And who knows, you parents might be paving the way for our next Neil Armstrong or John Glenn!

"This was a wonderful family team-building experience – and we got to press a lot of buttons."

Andy Zupan
Parent

"I really enjoyed myself. I didn't expect all the equipment. I first thought the sky is the limit. Now I know it's the galaxy."

Michael Abdul-Misih
Future Astronaut
Age 12

"The Bloomin' Festival
seeks to heighten
north Alabama's
community awareness
and interest in the arts."

Joyce Nix
Spokesperson
Saint Bernard Preparatory School

Bloomin' Festival
Cullman, Alabama

This event, held for over two decades, welcomes up to 25,000 visitors during the festival weekend. It showcases the community of Cullman and raises money for the local Saint Bernard Preparatory School. The festival is held on the school's uniquely scenic campus, located adjacent to the world-famous Ave Maria Grotto. The buildings surrounding the arts area are stone cut, multi-storied structures, some of which date back to the early 1800s. More than 150 artists from throughout the United States travel to Cullman every year to present a variety of wares and crafts. Unique garden art, handmade soap, hand-dyed fabrics, paintings, and sculptures are among the colorful selection of items sold at this increasingly popular two-day event. The arts are augmented with performances by musicians, children's activities, and a variety of Southern foods. This is a good festival for a good cause!

Great Moonbuggy Race
Huntsville, Alabama

Each year at the U.S. Space and Rocket Center, approximately 75 colleges and high schools compete in one of the most unusual races on the planet. The Great Moonbuggy Race is a competition that challenges students to design and build a human-powered, lightweight aluminum vehicle. All vehicles must carry simulated equipment and be capable of collapsing into a 4-foot square. Students race these vehicles one at a time over a half-mile obstacle course of simulated moonscape terrain. There are separate categories for colleges and high school teams, and teams must consist of one man and one woman. In addition to the first-place prize, students can also receive the "Best Engineering Design" award, a "Pits" award for ingenuity and persistence in overcoming problems, and a "Crash and Burn" award. The annual event is inspired by the actual lunar-roving vehicle project successfully completed at NASA's Marshall Space Flight Center in Huntsville during the 1960s and 1970s.

"Building a racing buggy gives the students hands-on experience that could pay off in fulfilling NASA's missions, as they become the next generation of engineers, scientists, and astronauts."

Angela Storey
Spokesperson
National Aeronautics and Space Administration

Art on the Lake
Guntersville, Alabama

For almost half a century, this arts and crafts fair has given Guntersville residents and visitors an opportunity to add a little pizazz to their home decor. With everything from framed watercolors to hand-thrown pottery, this waterside event donates its proceeds to sponsor college scholarships. With great deals and beautiful workmanship, these creations give local Tennessee Valley artists something to be proud of. Be sure to bring some cash, because plenty of fantastic art is available for purchase at this enjoyable event.

Artists, from top: Larry Allen, *Covered Jar*, 2004, Leeds, Alabama, LAPotter170@cs.com
Charles Holcomb, *Eagle*, 2004, Gadsden, Alabama, cbh7gk@bellsouth.net
Sharon Clay, *Prayerwear*, 2004-2005, Guntersville, Alabama, sharoneclay@bellsouth.net

Siege at Bridgeport
Civil War Reenactment
Bridgeport, Alabama

The Siege at Bridgeport Civil War Reenactment is held every March in northeast Alabama. It is reportedly the largest event of its kind in the state of Alabama, with more than 1,700 reenactors participating. The battle, which took place in April 1862, resulted in Union troops forcing Confederate soldiers to retreat across the Tennessee River back into Tennessee. Capturing the town eventually enabled the Union Army to resupply its troops in Chattanooga before they advanced into Georgia. This three-day event also involves hundreds of non-battle participants wearing period attire and includes a free fireworks display, numerous vendor tents, and a gala ball.

"We have grown from featuring a couple hundred participants to having over 1700 reenactors and 27 cannons. People really enjoy coming – we treat spectators and reenactors like family."

Glenn Hill
Reenactor Coordinator

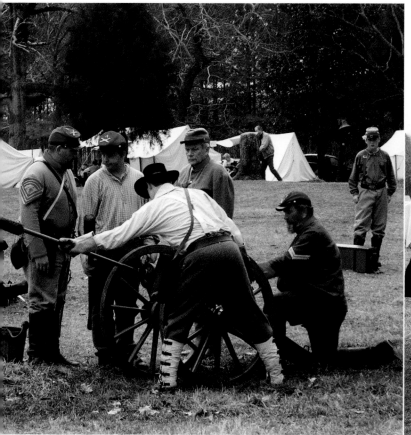

W.C. Handy Music Festival
Florence, Alabama

One of the Southeast's most popular summer celebrations is Florence's week-long W.C. Handy Music Festival. This event, usually held in late July or early August, honors William Christopher Handy, the world famous "Father of the Blues." Unlike many other large events held in one central location, this festival's performances are spread throughout the Shoals – at riverside parks, malls, restaurants, and theaters. Concerts, athletic events, Handy Nights, exhibits, and plays all highlight this festival. The W.C. Handy Music Festival has been recognized as one of the Southeast Tourism Society's *Top 20 Events* for more than two decades. For 25 years music enthusiasts have migrated from all over the country to enjoy and participate in this festival. Sponsored by the Music Preservation Society Inc., there are more than 100 scheduled events, most of which are free to the public. Many of the jazz and blues groups that perform are nationally known. You can also enjoy a host of special events, including the "Street Strut," numerous parades, jam sessions, and the "DaDooRunRun" for joggers and walkers.

"The texture of the blues is the sound of a sinner on revival day."

W.C. Handy
Blues Pioneer

"The W.C. Handy Music Festival is a hand-clappin', toe-tappin', street-struttin' week of music and events to celebrate the musical heritage of northwest Alabama and W.C. Handy, the father of the blues."

Nancy C. Gonce
Executive Director
W.C. Handy Music Festival

W.C. HANDY HOME & MUSEUM
620 W. COLLEGE ST.

Spirit of America
Decatur, Alabama

This Independence Day festival has all of the essential patriotic American ingredients, from snow cones and hot dogs to fireworks and rock 'n' roll. Held at Decatur's Point Mallard Park, the two-day event offers a multitude of games for kids, a diverse lineup of musical guests, a talent competition, and patriotic award ceremonies. Road races, amusement rides, and even the Miss Point Mallard Pageant are colorful additions to the festival. The celebration draws to a close with a dazzling fireworks display.

"Spirit of America is a one-stop place! Where else can you enjoy fair rides, fireworks, food, and a free concert?"

Wendy Black
Spokesperson
Spirit of America Festival

North Alabama Scottish Festival and Highland Games
Madison, Alabama

If you're eager to swap barbeque and fiddles for haggis and bagpipes, every year the city of Madison throws its annual North Alabama Scottish Festival and Highland Games. For years, this colorful festival has honored the many Scottish clans in the area. Don't expect to find the traditional, never-ending rows of hamburger and funnel cake stands at this festival. The event is pure Scottish – and proud of it! Each year, the organizers designate one person and one featured clan to be honored. A major emphasis of the festival is the display of traditional Scottish wares and memorabilia. You can also find entertainment every which way at this event. Observe border collies herding sheep and geese, enjoy traditional live music (from heritage pipes to folk singing), and see parades and Scottish dances of all sorts at this three-day event. Various Highland games such as the hammer toss, sheaf throwing, and the caber toss may be of special interest to those of you new to the traditional sporting events.

World's Longest Yard Sale

Kentucky, Tennessee, and Alabama

The slogan "shop till you drop" could have been coined for this four-day event traditionally held the first weekend in August. The especially enjoyable part of this sale is that the trail winds along 450 miles of back roads you most likely have never seen before. For almost 20 years, shoppers at this event have meandered through beautiful countrysides in search of treasures proudly displayed by residents from three different states. Front lawns are

often turned into showcases displaying everything from expensive antiques to who-knows-what. If you are looking for something out of the ordinary, you just might find it during this nationally known event. The sales route starts at U.S. Highway 127 in Covington, Kentucky, and goes through Tennessee to Lookout Mountain Parkway in Chattanooga. From there it goes on to U.S. Highway 157 and then to U.S. Highway 176, eventually ending in Gadsden, Alabama. To avoid traffic congestion, many shoppers prefer to enter the shopping route along the way rather than joining it at one of the starting points. Regardless of your style preferences, if you like rummaging for bargains, this is an event for you.

POINT OF BEGINNING
450 MILE OUTDOOR SALE
AUGUST 7TH THRU 10TH

Tanner's Tractor Pull

Tanner, Alabama

Tractor and truck pulls are held periodically throughout the Valley to the enthusiastic cheers of hundreds. The Alabamians of Tanner have been holding an annual tractor pull every summer for three decades. A tractor pull is a contest where both tractors and trucks compete to pull the heaviest load the longest distance. The competition generally occurs on dirt, and the load on the sled is dynamic – providing increasing resistance as time elapses. The two major components of a sled are the box and the pan. The pan increases friction with the track as the box, which is chain driven, comes forward toward the front of the sled. Inside the box are lead blocks – often weighing a combined 36,000 pounds or more. Both the competing tractors and trucks are high-powered state-of-the-art machines, and the power they generate is awesome. This event can at times be hard on the ears and produce whopping amounts of runaway air pollution, but it provides for a visceral, high-energy good time!

Big Spring Jam
Huntsville, Alabama

Al Green, the Allman Brothers, Lynyrd Skynyrd, and even George Clinton and the Parliament Funkadelic have all played Huntsville's Big Spring Jam. Since its inception in 1993, more than two million people have attended the Jam, which at present is averaging

more than 200,000 music-lovers per year. Named after scenic Big Spring Park, where the music festival takes place, the jam is full of excitement that lasts for three days (rain or shine) and is usually held in late September. Local businesses and organizations sponsor everything from karaoke competitions and food stands to tattoo parlors (of the temporary variety). Additional attractions include a 5K run, sumo-suit wrestling, and plenty of kid-friendly activities. The real reason to visit Big Spring Jam, however, is the music. In all, more than 70 different acts perform at the Jam, and event organizers make a great effort to book a diverse array of performers who entertain at the different stages around the park. Country artists, Christian artists, rock 'n' rollers, hip hop performers, and plenty of others manage to entertain visitors of all ages well after the sun goes down.

"Big Spring Jam is Huntsville's biggest party of the year!"

Kimball Lewis
Rock 'n' Roll Lover

Indian Burial Mounds Festival
Danville, Alabama

The Lawrence County Schools' Education Program sponsors this three-day annual festival, held each May at the Oakville Indian Mounds Education Center and Park about eight miles southeast of Moulton, Alabama. The festival features Indian dances, artwork, artifact exhibits, and numerous early-American craft demonstrations. This celebration also showcases Civil War actors and old weaponry and serves up plenty of history lessons along the way. Novelty concessions by independent vendors pepper the area, with early-American souvenirs available for purchase throughout the park. Canoeing, drumming, and Native American music also add to the enjoyable, unique atmosphere.

Old Time Fiddlers' Convention
Athens, Alabama

When Stephen Foster, who wrote "Oh! Susanna," penned that he "came from Alabama with a banjo on his knee," perhaps he was on his way back from the Old Time Fiddlers' Convention! Traditionally listed as a *Top 20 Event* in the Southeast, this convention is

unquestionably one of the most enjoyable festivals the Valley has to offer. It is held annually each October at Athens State University. The music generated here reflects not only the area's heritage, but also the true spirit of the Valley. Simply strolling through the campus gives you an appreciation of both the interesting people and the musical traditions that have contributed to the reputation of this festival. Hundreds of musicians from around the country meet for this two-day event, which includes everything from fiddling competitions for all ages (categories start at 10 and under), to singing and buck dancing. Groups can formally compete in any of the 15 events held in front of Founder's Hall and also participate in numerous informal jam sessions throughout the campus. And talk about a variety of musical instruments! Banjos, bass fiddles, guitars, dobros, autoharps, harmonicas, mandolins, dulcimers, washboards, spoons, and even washtubs are in abundance. Relax in a lawn chair and listen to the competition or visit the numerous vendors' exhibits. These exhibits, set up throughout the campus, often have instruments for sale. But regardless of whether you come to play, listen, learn, or shop, the experience is Tennessee Valley music at it purest.

"You usually see them in a circle under a shade tree. Expert or beginner, you're welcome to participate. There are no winners or losers, bosses or workers, just pickers having a great time."

Chuck Arnold
Bluegrass Musician

Riverfest Barbeque Cook-Off
Decatur, Alabama

Alabama barbeque lovers, listen up! For more than a decade, the Decatur Jaycees have hosted this annual weekend-long grilling competition, which has grown to feature more than 50 different teams. Competitors can enter their creations in numerous categories, including best sauce, chicken, ribs, pork, and brisket. Bands play a variety of music from jazz to classic rock, and the breeze off the water provides a delightful way to spend a September afternoon. Recognized by the state of Alabama as its official state barbeque championship, this event often has cooking teams staying overnight to ensure perfect culinary results. The competition's winners automatically qualify for the *American Royal World Championship Barbeque Cook-off* in Kansas City, Missouri. Funds raised by the Riverfest Barbeque Cook-Off are given to local, nonprofit charitable organizations.

"Riverfest is a whole lotta fun. So much good barbeque! And everyone thinks theirs is the best!

And they're all wrong, 'cause mine is."

Barry Sanders
Huntsville, Alabama

Harvest Festival

Boaz, Alabama

For more than 40 years, the citizens of Boaz have dusted off their overcoats and headed downtown for a two-day celebration of all things autumn and all things Boaz! Attendees can enjoy a top-notch classic car show, stock up on Christmas gifts from the slew of vendors selling crafts and wares of all varieties, and attend the Miss Harvest Festival Pageant. Plenty of live music fills the air, as do tempting aromas from the numerous food vendors. The festival includes a 5K run, a fairly involved kids' entertainment area, and a folk-life tent. This festival provides a great opportunity to purchase home decorations and knickknacks, so be sure to bring along a little extra cash. Whether you attend the celebration to eat boiled peanuts, purchase college football merchandise, sit in handmade rocking chairs, or just stroll about in the crisp October air, the Harvest Festival provides for a fun, upbeat day on the town.

Racking Horse World Celebration
Priceville, Alabama

More than 2,000 horses and owners compete in approximately 150 classes during this eight-day celebration. The events and festivities take place annually in late September at the Celebration Arena in Priceville, Alabama. Racking horses (dubbed the "poor man's walking horse") and their riders are cheered on at this event by more than 100,000 people. The Celebration also features other festivities such as dog contests, which are popular with many visitors. Going strong for more than three decades, the Celebration is sponsored by the Racking Horse Breeders Association of America (RHBAA) and involves juvenile, amateur, and professional riders from all across the country.

So what the heck's the difference between a *walking* horse and a *racking* horse?

Many folks know that Tennessee is famous for its walking horses and that it hosts the World Celebration in Shelbyville every year. Others are familiar with the lesser-known racking horse, which receives its very own annual celebration in Priceville, Alabama. The major difference between the two horses is their gait. Racking horses only allow one foot to strike the ground at a time. The "rack" of the racking horse is a bilateral four-beat gait, which cannot be described as being either a pace or a trot. The Tennessee walking horse, on the other hand, generally performs three distinct gaits – either the flat-foot walk, the running walk, or the canter. To discover more about these differences, why not swing by Priceville and Shelbyville and learn first-hand!

Seafood Festival
Guntersville, Alabama

This annual festival is sponsored by the local St. William Catholic Church and serves up more than its share of fish, shrimp, crab, crawfish, hush puppies, and slaw. Located on the breezy shores of Guntersville lake, this festival also features numerous craft vendors. You can find a variety of wares ranging from beautiful Mexican pottery to great-smelling handmade soaps. Sit back and enjoy the live music or, of you're feeling brave, attempt a harnessed ascent up a climbing wall.

Alabama Gourd Festival
Cullman, Alabama

Held every third weekend in October, this popular event could just as easily be called a festival of arts. That is because the numerous vendor booths feature amazing arts and crafts made from the common gourd. If you have ever had any interest in how gourds are decorated, you need to attend this two-day event, which sponsors a multitude of gourd art-crafting classes for young and old alike. The festival is sponsored by the Alabama Gourd Society (ALGS), whose objective is the promotion of the culture and crafting of gourds. Live music and food are available but simply do not compare to viewing the gorgeous gourds on display. And if you'd like to try decorating a gourd at home, there are plenty of "raw" gourds available for you to purchase.

"The annual gourd festival promotes the culture and crafting of gourds as an informational and educational service to the Alabama Gourd Society members and the public."

Glenn Burkhalter
Former President
Alabama Gourd Society

Alabama Renaissance Faire
Florence, Alabama

Hear ye, hear ye! All Valley-area knights, maidens, and trolls should read carefully. Florence hosts this colorful event every October, and presenters and guests alike attend in splendid fashion. Swords, girdles, chain mail, shields, and jewel-encrusted crowns all contribute to the very ornate, unique period costumes exhibited by many of this festival's attendees. The Faire attempts (quite successfully) to capture the essence of what life was like during the time period between the 12th and 16th centuries. Expect to see fencing demonstrations, weapons displays, dancing, theatrical performances, and more. Minstrels are scattered throughout the area, playing tunes on dulcimers, mandolins, and flutes. Fortunately, the vendors (who sell everything from walking staffs to chicken-on-a-stick) accept 21st-century currency!

"The participants put so much darn effort into their costumes and demonstrations that it is quite hard not to really be impressed."

**Matt Turner
Faire Attendee**

Trail of Tears
Commemorative Motorcycle Ride
Tennessee and Alabama

The Trail of Tears Commemorative Motorcycle Ride is held every third Saturday in September, and riders from throughout the United States journey to the Tennessee Valley to make this ride. The trail winds from Chattanooga, Tennessee, to the Florence and Waterloo area in Alabama, and is considered the world's largest motorcycle ride. In the past, and depending upon the weather, this ride has had up to 130,000 participants. Many ride the entire distance, while others simply traverse a section thereof. Thousands of people line the route of this well-organized event to see the riders with their different types of flags cruise down the road. Participation in the ride is free, and designated merchandise vendors are scattered along the way, selling a variety of items. Part of the profits go to scholarships for American Indian students in Alabama and Tennessee. More than 100 highway signs identify the travel corridor for participants and spectators alike. This impressive event reminds us of a tragic decision by the U.S. government, which affected thousands of Native Americans living in the Tennessee Valley almost 170 years ago.

"We tried to replicate the Indians' voyage by motorcycles

with a goal of getting 4,000 riders to honor

the deaths of the Native Americans who died on that journey.

Since then, we have far exceeded that goal."

Bill Casom
Original Event Organizer (1994)
Chattanooga, Tennessee

TRAIL OF TEARS

In May 1838 soldiers under the command of Gen. Winfield Scott began rounding up Cherokee Indians in this area who had refused to move to Indian Territory (Oklahoma). About 15,000 Cherokees were placed in stockades in Tennessee and Alabama until their removal. Roughly 3,000 were sent by boat down the Tennessee River and the rest were marched overland in the fall and winter of 1838-39. This forced removal under harsh conditions resulted in the deaths of about 4,000 Cherokees.

In late June 1838 a party of 1,070 poorly equipped Indians was marched overland from Ross' Landing at Chattanooga, TN to Waterloo, AL because of low water in the upper Tennessee River. Following the general route of present-day U.S. Hwy. 72, they camped at Bolivar, Bellefonte, and Woodville (Jackson County). About 300 escaped along the way and, at Bellefonte on June 26, the remainder refused to proceed. The local militia under the command of Army Capt. G. S. Drane was called out to get the group started and escort it to Waterloo. Arriving in miserable condition on July 10, 1838, the Cherokees were placed on boats to continue their journey west.

The "Trail of Tears", which resulted from the Indian Removal Act passed by the U.S. Congress in 1830, is one of the darkest chapters in American history.

This route was designated as the "Trail of Tears Corridor of North Alabama" by resolution of the Alabama Legislature on July 13, 1995. Alabama remains the home of many Cherokee Indians today.

SPONSORED BY: TRAIL OF TEARS CORRIDOR COMMITTEE OF ALABAMA
ALABAMA WATERFOWL ASSOCIATION

The Living Christmas Tree
Huntsville, Alabama

For more than 20 years, First Baptist Church of Huntsville has presented The Living Christmas Tree as an annual gift to the city and the surrounding areas of north Alabama and south-central Tennessee. Weighing 6,000 pounds, the "tree" supports more than 150 singers accompanied by a full orchestra. The interior of the tree structure includes air conditioning to cool the singers during the performances. The tree, topped off with a 6-foot star, stands 40 feet tall and includes 455 miniature lights. All of this results in a magnificent image for the thousands of guests who attend this holiday performance. There are nightly performances for several days prior to Christmas. Attendance is free, and no offerings are taken at any of the performances. This unique presentation truly puts people in the mood for the Christmas season!

Valley Geocaching
Alabama and Tennessee

Enjoyable outdoor activities can be somewhat sparse in the colder months. Fortunately for local outdoor enthusiasts, the sport of geocaching has caught on in the region in recent years. This is a particularly good hobby for winter or spring, due to diminished interference by trees and over-hanging foliage. Geocaching is an international adventure game for global positioning system (GPS) users. All you need is a GPS unit (averaging between $100 and $250 at outdoor stores) and a sense of adventure! The goal is to find a treasure ("cache"), which will usually be a box containing hidden trinkets. If you find the box and take a trinket, you simply replace it with another one. The treasures may be hidden on trails, inside caves, in trees, or just about anywhere. To begin, simply log onto www.geocaching.com, enter the destination area's zip code, and download a set of coordinates to enter into your GPS unit. Then the hunt begins! Thousands of caches are hidden in north Alabama and middle Tennessee. Just pick up a GPS, decide where you want to go exploring, and input the information. Happy geocaching!

Polar Bears Club New Year's Dip
Decatur, Alabama

As if January wasn't cold enough already! Each New Year's Day at the Decatur Riverwalk Marina, members of the Decatur Polar Bears Club start off the new year with a refreshing dip in the Tennessee River. Folks of all ages line up along the public dock for an exhilarating – and very brief – swim to welcome in 12 new months. Regardless of the weather or water temperature, the Club has made this an annual event for more than 20 years. This is not an overly involved organizational process. Folks just show up, muster as much courage as possible, and take the plunge. If, on January 1, you find yourself recovering from a New Year's Eve party hangover, this could be the answer. Just bring along a towel and some hot coffee!

"It's a lot more fun than watching football all New Year's Day."

Wayne Holliday
Original Event Organizer (1985)
Decatur, Alabama

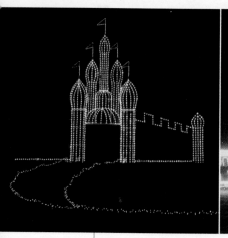

The Galaxy of Lights
Huntsville, Alabama

Consistently named to the Southeast Tourism Society's *Top 20 Events*, this is one of north Alabama's most popular holiday traditions. Held annually between Thanksgiving and New Year's Eve, the Huntsville Botanical Garden's Galaxy of Lights is a stunning two-mile-long winter wonderland featuring larger-than-life animated light displays. With assistance and displays from numerous organizations around Huntsville, the Garden presents beautiful lighted presentations of both traditional holiday scenes as well as characters from nursery rhymes. The Galaxy is a perfect treat for anyone in search of holiday cheer!

"This two-mile drive through our holiday light extravaganza has garnered national recognition by being named to the Southeastern Tourism Society's Top 20 Events six years in a row. There's just so much to see that it's no wonder that the Galaxy of Lights has become the Tennessee Valley's favorite holiday tradition."

Stephanie Hudson
Special Events Coordinator
Huntsville Botanical Garden

Getting in the Spirit
Throughout the Valley

Few things get the entire family in the holiday mood like climbing into the van and heading out to a Christmas tree farm to pick and cut the family tree. Real, freshly-cut trees are still the nation's favorite holiday decoration. It is estimated that Americans purchase nearly 30 million live Christmas trees during the holidays, with up to 30 percent of the trees being bought from a "choose-and-cut" farm. Christmas tree farms (of which there are approximately 5,000 in the country) first sprang up during the Great Depression. Nurserymen couldn't sell their evergreens for landscaping, so they cut them for use as Christmas trees. Cultivated trees were preferred because they have more symmetrical shapes than wild ones. Six species account for about 90 percent of the nation's Christmas tree trade. Scotch pine ranks first, comprising about 40 percent of the market, followed by Douglas fir, which accounts for about 35 percent. The other big sellers are Noble fir, White pine, Balsam fir and White spruce. In the Deep South, both the Leland Cypress and the traditional Virginia pines prove to be two of the most popular trees. Regardless of the type, size, or cost of your tree, it is guaranteed that the family – even the dog – will have a good time outdoors. Comparing and debating which tree to select is all part of the fun.

"A natural Christmas tree brings home the true spirit of Christmas and reminds the family of what's important by the sight and smell of a fresh tree."

Rodger Schwerman
Schwerman Christmas Tree Plantation
Laceys Spring, Alabama

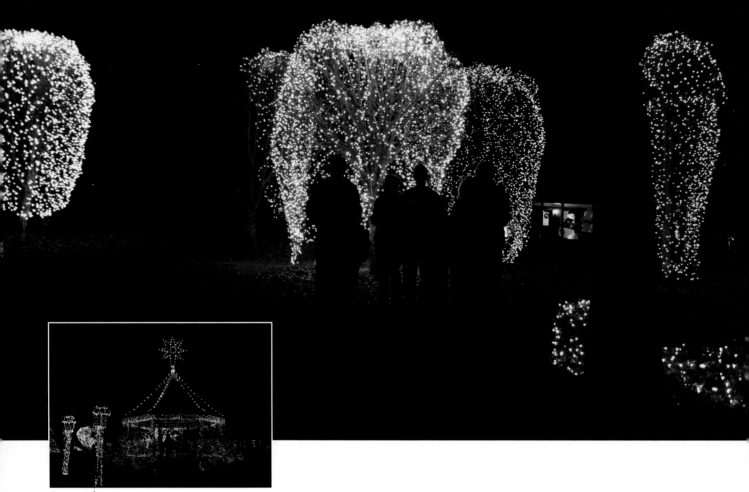

Christmas in the Park
Arab, Alabama

Every year on the Friday following Thanksgiving, the city of Arab kicks off its month-long Christmas in the Park holiday event with a lighting ceremony. This enjoyable happening features everything from live Christmas music to hot chocolate. More than 1,500,000 twinkling lights illuminate Arab City Park, to the enjoyment of bundled-up attendees. Festivities continue every weekend up until Christmas Day, and visitors from all over the area drop by this winter wonderland if only to stroll through the park after sunset. Admission is not charged, but donations are accepted. Christmas in the Park even features a drop-off box for letters to a certain jolly ol' elf. Arab's Historic Complex, located adjacent to the park, also gets into the festive yuletide swing of things. These historic buildings, which include a church, school, general store, and an operational grist-mill, have been relocated to the site, adorned with Christmas decorations, and restored to look the way they did a century ago.

"Christmas in the Park has become a family tradition for thousands, and the Lighting Ceremony is a special way for them to end their Thanksgiving festivities and begin planning for upcoming Christmas gatherings. For a truly inspiring Christmas experience, you won't want to miss this event!"

Becky Hawkins
Coordinator
Christmas in the Park

Eagle Awareness Program
Guntersville, Alabama

In 1782, the founding fathers chose the bald eagle to be the national bird of the United States. The word "bald" does not mean that the bird has no feathers. Instead, it comes from the word "piebald," an old word meaning "marked with white." For over two decades, the Lake Guntersville State Park has proudly held the Eagle Awareness Program. This event features speakers and guides who lead eagle-watching tours and hold discussions about the indigenous bald eagle population in the area. The program is held for several weekends each January and consists of both early morning and late afternoon eagle-watching field trips. Each trip lasts approximately an hour and a half and provides an educational outdoor experience for nature lovers of all ages.

Santa's Village
Huntsville, Alabama

During the holidays, Huntsville's Constitution Village is transformed into a child's winter wonderland and is beautifully decked out with displays of Christmas lights, candy canes, animated dolls, brightly wrapped presents, whimsical displays, and a variety of beautiful "little elves." Sponsored by both the EarlyWorks Museum Complex and the Alabama Constitution Village Foundation, children of all ages get to visit Santa in his home, check out his Toy Shop, and pet live reindeer in their stable. Kids can also meet numerous characters such as Santa's elves, Frosty the Snowman, and the Gingerbread Man. Santa's Village features a Toymaker's Workshop, an Elf's Candy Kitchen, and many activities for the young and young at heart. Entertainment is present nightly and includes local musicians, dancers, carolers, and performing school groups. Open for almost an entire month prior to Christmas and manned by volunteers, the Village welcomes school groups during the day and the general public in the evenings. Upwards of 30,000 people regularly visit this magical setting every holiday season – and there are many good reasons why.

CHAPTER IX:
Looking Back and Traveling Forward
A Little Philosophy

The Tennessee Valley has a long and colorful history. No matter how you define the geographic parameters of the Valley, the region and the Tennessee River have witnessed a variety of challenges and changes. How much of the Valley's commerce and outdoor recreational activities can be directly attributed to the river is subject to debate. However, you can be sure that the river has played a major role in the development of communities and life throughout the Valley.

Hal Borland, naturalist and outdoor writer for *The New York Times*, once stated, "Any river is really the summation of the whole valley. To think of it as nothing but water is to ignore the greater part." In the Tennessee Valley, this "greater part" consists of beautiful mountains, lakes, rolling hills and cotton fields. It also consists of a populace whose demographics reflect nationalities and cultures of many origins.

While we take great pride in pointing to the area's industrial and economic progress, we must never overlook the fact that the Valley's history, culture, and time-honored customs must be preserved for our children and grandchildren. It is important that residents and visitors alike make every effort to visit its attractions, events, and local festivals. Chambers of commerce and local convention and visitors bureaus have a wealth of information on activities throughout the year. A multitude of festivals and attractions eagerly await you! Many of these functions are not only entertaining for the entire family, but are often unique to the Valley. Taking your loved ones to one of these events may well turn out to be the educational or social experience of the year.

It is also important to ensure that regional symbols – from foods and music to antebellum-style architecture and cultural idiosyncracies – do not dissappear with the passage of time. The same holds true for our traditions. From outdoor family reunions and cemetery "Decoration Days" to old-fashioned river baptisms, these activities are special to this part of the country and must be appreciated and preserved whenever possible.

This book and the story of the Tennessee Valley and its people are not finished, nor will they ever be. There are too many wonderful places to explore and subjects to write about. Just head down a country road and see what awaits. Perhaps you can add a few chapters and build a few memories of your own. Hopefully this book – and the contact information on the following pages – will assist you in your travels and experiences. Good luck, and have fun!

"The American South is a geographical entity, a historical fact, a place in the imagination, and the homeland for an array of Americans who consider themselves Southerners. The region is often shrouded in romance and myth, but its realities are as intriguing, as intricate, as its legends."

Bill Ferris, Ph.D.
Coeditor
Encyclopedia of Southern Culture

APPENDIX:
Tennessee Valley Contact Information

Selected Tennessee Chambers of Commerce

Bell Buckle Chamber of Commerce	www.bellbucklechamber.com	931-389-9663	P.O. Box 222 Bell Buckle, TN 37020
Bledsoe County Chamber of Commerce	www.bledsoechamber.com	423-447-2791	P.O. Box 205 Pikeville, TN 37367
Cannon County Chamber of Commerce	www.cannontn.com	615-563-2222	313 W. Main St. Woodbury, TN 37190
Cookville Area-Putnam County Chamber of Commerce	www.cookevillechamber.com	931-526-2211 800-264-5541	Town Centre, 1 W. First St. Cookeville, TN 38501
DeKalb County Chamber of Commerce	www.smithvilletn.com	615-597-4163	301 N. Public Square P.O. Box 64, Smithville, TN 37166
Dickson County Chamber of Commerce	www.dicksoncountychamber.com	615-446-2349	119 Highway 70 E. Dickson, TN 37055-2080
Fayetteville and Lincoln County Chamber of Commerce	www.vallnet.com/chamberofcommerce	931-433-1234 888-433-1238	208 S. Elk Ave. P.O. Box 515, Fayetteville, TN 37334
Franklin County Chamber of Commerce	www.franklincountychamber.com	931-967-6788	44 Chamber Way P.O. Box 280, Winchester, TN 37398
Giles County Chamber of Commerce and Tourism	www.gilescountychamber.com	931-363-3789	110 N. Second St. Pulaski, TN 38478
Hickman County Chamber of Commerce	www.hickmanco.com/chamber	931-729-5774	P.O. Box 126 Centerville, TN 37033
Humphreys County Chamber of Commerce	www.waverly.net/hcchamber	931-296-4865	124 E. Main St. P.O. Box 733, Waverly, TN 37185
Lawrence County Chamber of Commerce	www.chamberofcommerce.lawrence.tn.us	931-762-4911 877-388-4911	1609 N. Locust Ave. P.O. Box 86, Lawrenceburg, TN 38464
Lewis County Chamber of Commerce	www.lewiscountychamber.com	931-796-4084	112 E. Main St. Hohenwald, TN 38462
Lynchburg Moore County Chamber of Commerce	www.lynchburgtenn.com	931-759-4111	P.O. Box 421 Lynchburg, TN 37352
Manchester Area Chamber of Commerce	www.macoc.org	931-728-7635	110 E. Main St. Manchester, TN 37355
Marion County Chamber of Commerce	www.marioncountychamber.com	423-942-5103	302 Betsy Pack Drive, Jasper, TN 37347
Marshall County Chamber of Commerce	www.marshallchamber.org	931-359-3863	227 Second Ave. N. Lewisburg, TN 37091
Perry County Chamber of Commerce	www.perrycountytennessee.com	931-589-2166	P.O. Box 16 Linden, TN 37096
Rutherford County Chamber of Commerce	www.rutherfordchamber.org	615-893-6565 800-716-7560	501 Memorial Blvd., P.O. Box 864 Murfreesboro, TN 37133-0864
Sequatchie County Chamber of Commerce	www.sequatchie.com	423-949-7608	13 Rankin Ave. N., P.O. Box 1653 Dunlap, TN 37327
Shelbyville-Bedford County Chamber of Commerce	www.shelbyvilletn.com	931-684-3482 888-662-2525	100 N. Cannon Blvd. Shelbyville, TN 37160
Tullahoma Area Chamber of Commerce	www.tullahoma.org	931-455-5497	P.O. Box 1205 Tullahoma, TN 37388

Van Buren County Chamber of Commerce	www.vanburenchamber.com	931-946-7033	P.O. Box 814 Spencer, TN 38585
Wartrace Chamber of Commerce	www.wartracechamber.org	931-389-9999	P.O. Box 543 Wartrace, TN 37183
Wayne County Chamber of Commerce	www.waynecountychamber.org	931-722-9022	303 Courthouse P.O. Box 675, Waynesboro, TN 38485
Williamson County-Franklin Chamber of Commerce	www.williamson-franklinchamber.com	615-794-1225 800-356-3445	P.O. Box 156 Franklin, TN 37065

Selected Tennessee Tourism Bureaus

Chattanooga Area Convention and Visitors Bureau	www.chattanoogafun.com	423-756-8687 800-322-3344	2 Broad St. Chattanooga, TN 37402
Hamilton County Parks and Recreation	www.hamiltontn.gov/parks	423-842-0177	2318 Gold Point Circle Hixon, TN 37343
Hardin County Convention and Visitors Bureau	www.tourhardincounty.org	731-925-8181 800-552-3866	495 Main St Savannah, TN 38372
Lawrence County Tourism Department	www.chamberofcommerce.lawrence.tn.us /tourism.php	931-762-3733	1 Public Square Lawrenceburg, TN 38464
Middle East Tennessee Tourism Council	www.vacationeasttennessee.org	865-777-2606 800-440-0447	10205 S. River Trail Knoxville, TN 37922
Middle Tennessee Tourism Council	www.middletennesseetourism.com	615-862-8828	501 Union St., Sixth Floor Nashville, TN 37219-1705
Middle Tennessee Convention and Visitors Bureau	www.visitplantations.com	931-381-7176 800-381-1865	8 Public Square Columbia, TN 38401
Nashville Convention and Visitors Bureau	www.nashvillecvb.com	615-259-4700 800-657-6910	One Nashville Place, 150 Fourth Ave. N. Suite G-250, Nashville, TN 37219
Rhea Economic and Tourism Council	www.rheacountyetc.com	423-775-6171	107 Main St., Dayton, TN 37321
South Central Tennessee Tourism Association	www.sctta.com	931-363-3606	2018 Joann Road Pulaski, TN 38478
Southeast Tennessee Tourism Association	www.southeasttennessee.com	423-424-4263	P.O. Box 4757 Chattanooga, TN 37405
Tennessee Department of Tourist Development	www.tnvacation.com	615-741-9001 800-462-8366	312 Eighth Ave. N. 25th Floor, Nashville, TN 37243
Tennessee Department of Tourism	www.state.tn.us/tourdev	615-741-2158 800-836-6200	P.O. Box 23170 Nashville, TN 37202
Tourism Association of Southwest Tennessee	www.tast.tn.org	731-616-7474 866-261-7534	P.O. Box 10543 Jackson, TN 38308
Williamson County Convention and Visitors Bureau	www.williamsoncvb.org	615-794-1225 800-356-3445	P.O. Box 156 Franklin, TN 37065
Wilson County Convention and Visitors Bureau	www.wilsoncountycvb.com	615-453-9655 800-789-1327	233 E. Gay St., Court House Annex Lebanon, TN 37087

Selected Tennessee Attractions and Locations

Adventure Science Center	www.adventuresci.com	615-862-5160	800 Fort Negley Blvd. Nashville, TN 37203
Battles for Chattanooga Museum	www.battlesforchattanooga.com	423-821-2812	1110 E. Brow Road Lookout Mountain, TN 37350
Bluff View Art District	www.bluffviewartdistrict.com	423-265-5033 800-725-8338	411 E. Second St. Chattanooga, TN 37403

Buford Pusser Home and Museum	www.talentondisplay.com/pusser.html	731-632-4080	342 Pusser St. Adamsville, TN 38310
Carnton Plantation	www.carnton.org	615-794-0903	1345 Carnton Lane Franklin, TN 37064
Carter House	www.carter-house.org	615-791-1861	P.O. Box 555 Franklin, TN 37065
Chattanooga African-American Museum	www.caamhistory.com	423-266-8658	200 E. Martin Luther King Blvd. Chattanooga, TN 37403
Chattanooga Market	www.chattanoogamarket.com	423-266-9270	1826 Carter St., P.O. Box 11123 Chattanooga, TN 37401
Chickamauga & Chattanooga National Military Park	www.nps.gov/chch	423-821-4224	110 Point Park Road Lookout Mountain, TN 37350
Coolidge Park	www.chattanooga.gov	423-643-6050	150 River St. Chattanooga, TN 37405
Country Music Hall of Fame and Museum	www.countrymusichalloffame.com	615-416-2001 800-852-6437	222 Fifth Ave. S. Nashville, TN 37203
Creative Discovery Museum	www.cdmfun.org	423-756-2738	321 Chestnut St. Chattanooga, TN 37402
Cumberlands Craft Trail	www.craftstrail.com	800-235-9073 615-563-2787	P.O. Box 111 Woodbury, TN 37190
Cumberland Trail	www.cumberlandtrail.org	931-456-6259	19 E. Fourth St. Crossville, TN 38555
Downtown Lynchburg	www.lynchburgtenn.com	931-759-4111	P.O. Box 421 Lynchburg, TN 37352
Elk River Canoe Rental	www.elkrivercanoes.com	931-937-6886 877-355-2266	190 Smithland Road Kelso, TN 37348
Fall Creek Falls State Park	state.tn.us/environment/parks/ fallcreekfalls	423-881-5298	2009 Village Camp Road, Route 3 Box 300, Pikeville, TN 37367-9803
Falls Mill	www.fallsmill.com	931-469-7161	134 Falls Mill Road Belvidere, TN 37306
Glory Land Road	www.southeasttennessee.com	423-424-4263	P.O. Box 4757 Chattanooga, TN 37405
Grand Ole Opry and Museum	www.opry.com	615-871-6779 800-733-6779	2804 Opryland Drive Nashville, TN 37214
The Hermitage	www.thehermitage.com	615-889-2941	4580 Rachel's Lane Nashville, TN 37076
Hunter Museum of American Art	www.huntermuseum.org	423-267-0968	10 Bluff View Chattanooga, TN 37403-1197
Incline Railway	www.lookoutmountain.com	423-821-4224	827 E. Brow Road Lookout Mountain, TN 37350
Jack Daniel's Distillery	www.jackdaniels.com	931-759-6180	Jack Daniel's Visitor Center Lynchburg, TN 37352
Lookout Mountain	www.lookoutmountain.com	800-825-8366	P.O. Box 2315 Chattanooga, TN 37409
Lookout Mountain Flight Park	www.hangglide.com	706-398-3541 800-688-5637	7201 Scenic Highway Rising Fawn, GA 30738
Nashville Zoo	www.nashvillezoo.org	615-833-1534	3777 Nolensville Road Nashville, TN 37211
Natchez Trace Parkway	www.scenictrace.com	662-680-4027 800-305-7417	2680 Natchez Trace Parkway Tupelo, MS 38801

Old Stone Fort State Park	www.state.tn.us	931-723-5073	732 Stone Fort Drive Manchester, TN 37355
Parthenon	www.parthenon.org	615-862-8431	Centennial Park Office Nashville, TN 37201
Point Park	www.nps.gov/chch	423-821-7786	110 Point Park Road Lookout Mountain, TN 37350
Rock City	www.seerockcity.com	706-820-2531 800-854-0675	1400 Patten Road Chattanooga, TN 37350
Ruby Falls	www.rubyfalls.com	423-821-2544	1720 S. Scenic Highway Chattanooga, TN 37409
Ryman Auditorium	www.ryman.com	615-458-8700	116 Fifth Ave. N. Nashville, TN 37219
Shiloh National Military Park	www.shilohbattlefield.org	731-689-5275	1055 Pittsburg Landing Road Shiloh, TN 38376
Southern Belle	www.chattanoogariverboat.com	423-266-4488 800-766-2784	201 Riverfront Parkway, Pier 2 Chattanooga, TN 37402-1616
Stones River National Battlefield	www.nps.gov/stri	615-893-9501	3501 Old Nashville Highway Murfreesboro, TN 37129
Tennessee Antebellum Trail	www.antebellumtrail.com	800-381-1865	636 Farrell Parkway Nashville, TN 37220
Tennessee Aquarium	www.tnaqua.org	423-265-0698 800-262-0695	One Broad St. Chattanooga, TN 37401-2048
Tennessee River Museum	www.tourhardincounty.org/trm.htm	800-552-3866	495 Main St. Savannah, TN 38372
Tennessee Sports Hall of Fame and Museum	www.tshf.net	615-242-4750 888-846-8384	501 Broadway Nashville, TN 37203
Tennessee State Museum	www.tnmuseum.org	615-741-2692 800-407-4324	505 Deaderick St. Nashville, TN 37243
University of the South	www.sewanee.edu	931-598-1286	735 University Ave. Sewanee, TN 37383
Walking The District	www.thedistrictnashville.org	615-244-4911 800-657-6910	144 Second Ave. N. Suite 200, Nashville, TN 37201

Selected Tennessee Festivals and Events

Battle of Franklin Civil War Reenactment	www.battleoffranklin.com	615-794-1225 800-356-3445	P.O. Box 156 Franklin, TN 37065
Bonnaroo	www.bonnaroo.com	931-728-7635	110 E. Main St. Manchester, TN 37355
CMA Music Festival	www.cmafest.com	800-262-3378	One Music Circle S. Nashville, TN 37203
Dickens of a Christmas	www.historicfranklin.com	615-591-8500	510 Columbia Ave Franklin, TN 37064
Gaylord Opryland at Christmastime	www.gaylordhotels.com/gaylordopryland	866-972-6779	2800 Opryland Drive Nashville, TN 37214
Goats, Music and More	www.goatsmusicandmore.com	931-359-1544	131 E. Church St., P.O. Box 1968 Lewisburg, TN 37091
Jack Daniel's World Championship Inv. Barbecue	www.jackdaniels.com	931-759-6180	Jack Daniel's Visitor Center Lynchburg, TN 37352
Lincoln County Fair	www.lincolncountyfairinfo.com	931-433-1234 888-433-1238	208 S. Elk Ave., P.O. Box 515 Fayetteville, TN 37334

Mule Day	www.muleday.com	931-381-9557	P.O. Box 66 Columbia TN 38402
Nashville Lawn and Garden Show	www.nashvillelawnandgardenshow.com	615-876-7680	P.O. Box 247 Whites Creek, TN 37189
National Cornbread Festival	www.nationalcornbread.com	423-837-0022	P.O. Box 247 South Pittsburg, TN 37380
Pumpkin Harvest Festival	www.waynecountychamber.org	931-722-9022	303 Courthouse, P.O. Box 675 Waynesboro, TN 38485
Railroad Rendezvous Springfest	www.rrspringfest.com	931-526-2211 800-264-5541	Town Centre, 1 W. First St. Cookeville, TN 38501
RC Cola and MoonPie Festival	www.bellbucklechamber.com	931-389-6547	P.O. Box 222 Bell Buckle, TN 37020
Riverbend Festival	www.riverbendfestival.com	423-756-2211	180 Hamm Road Chattanooga, TN 37405
Rock City's Enchanted Garden of Lights	www.seerockcity.com	706-820-2531 800-854-0675	1400 Patten Road Chattanooga, TN 37350
Scopes Monkey Trial	www.rheacountyetc.com/chamber/scopes	423-775-7801	107 Main St. Dayton, TN 37321
Shadow Valley Gospel Music Festival	www.singingambassadors.com	931-438-0307	P.O. Box 179 Fayetteville, TN 37334-0179
Sorghum Squeeze Festival	N/A	931-294-2154	296 Burnt Hill Road Unionville, TN 37180
Southern Brewer's Festival	www.southernbrewersfest.org	423-267-2739	222 Broad St. Chattanooga, TN 37402
Tennessee Arts and Crafts Association Spring Fair	www.tennesseecrafts.org	615-385-1904	P.O. Box 120066 Nashville, TN 37212-0066
Tennessee History Festival	www.state.tn.us/environment/parks/parks/Bicentennial	615-741-5280	600 James Robertson Parkway Nashville, TN 37243-3081
Tennessee State Fairgrounds December Flea Market	www.tennesseestatefair.org	615-862-8980	P.O. Box 40208 Nashville, TN 37204
Tennessee Titans Football	www.titansonline.com	615-565-4200	The Coliseum, One Titans Way Nashville, TN 37213
Tennessee Walking Horse National Celebration	www.twhnc.com	931-684-5915 888-662-2525	P.O. Box 1010 Shelbyville, TN 37162

Selected Alabama Chambers of Commerce

Albertville Chamber of Commerce	www.cityofalbertville.com	256-878-3821 800-878-3821	P.O. Box 1457 Albertville, AL 35950
Arab Chamber of Commerce	www.arabcity.org	256-586-3138 888-403-2722	1157 N. Main St. Arab, AL 35016
Ardmore AL/TN Chamber of Commerce	www.ardmorechamberofcommerce.com	256-423-7588	P.O. Box 845 Ardmore, TN 38449
Athens-Limestone County Chamber of Commerce	www.tourathens.com	256-232-2600	101 S. Beaty St., P.O. Box 150 Athens, AL 35612
Blount County-Oneonta Chamber of Commerce	www.blountoneontachamber.org	205-274-2153	227 Second Ave. E., P.O. Box 1487 Oneonta, AL 35121
Boaz Chamber of Commerce	www.boazchamberofcommerce.com	256-593-8154 800-746-2629	100 E. Bartlett Ave. Boaz, AL 35957
Cherokee County Chamber of Commerce	www.cherokee-chamber.org	256-927-8455	801 Cedar Bluff Road P.O. Box 86, Centre, AL 35960

Cullman Area Chamber of Commerce	www.cullmanchamber.org	256-734-0454 800-313-5114	301 Second Ave. S.W. P.O. Box 1104, Cullman, AL 35056
Decatur-Morgan County Chamber of Commerce	www.dcc.org	256-353-5312	515 Sixth Ave. N.E. Decatur, AL 35602
Fort Payne Chamber of Commerce	www.fortpayne.org	256-845-2741	300 Gault Ave. N. P.O. Box 680125, Fort Payne, AL 35968
Franklin County Chamber of Commerce	www.franklincountychamber.org	256-332-1760	103 N. Jackson Ave. P.O. Box 44, Russellville, AL 35653
Gadsden Area Chamber of Commerce	www.gadsdenchamber.com	256-543-3472 800-238-6924	One Commerce Square P.O. Box 185, Gadsden, AL 35902
Grant Chamber of Commerce	www.grantchamberofcommerce.com	256-728-8800	P.O. Box 221 Grant, AL 35747
Greater Jackson County Chamber of Commerce	www.jacksoncountychamber.com	256-259-5500 800-259-5508	407 E. Willow St. Scottsboro, AL 35768
Hamilton Area Chamber of Commerce	www.cityofhamilton.org	205-921-7786	P.O. Box 1168 Hamilton, AL 35570
Hartselle Area Chamber of Commerce	www.hartsellechamber.com	256-773-4370 800-294-0692	110 Railroad St. S.W. P.O. Box 817, Hartselle, AL 35640
Huntsville-Madison County Chamber of Commerce	www.hsvchamber.org	256-535-2000	225 Church St. Huntsville, AL 35801
Lake Guntersville Chamber of Commerce	www.lakeguntersville.org	256-582-3612 800-869-5253	200 Gunter Ave. P.O. Box 577, Guntersville, AL 35976
Lawrence County Chamber of Commerce	www.lawrencealabama.com	256-974-1658	12001 Alabama Highway 157 P.O. Box 325, Moulton, AL 35650
Madison Chamber of Commerce	www.madisonalchamber.com	256-461-0518	P.O. Box 1065 Madison, AL 35758
Rainsville Chamber of Commerce	www.rainsvillealabama.com	256-638-7800	P.O. Box 396 Rainsville, AL 35986
Shoals Chamber of Commerce	www.shoalschamber.com	256-764-4661 877-764-4661	612 S. Court St. P.O. Box 1331, Florence, AL 35630

Selected Alabama Tourism Bureaus

Alabama Bureau of Tourism and Travel	www.touralabama.org	334-242-4169 800-252-2262	401 Adams Ave., Suite 126 P.O. Box 4927, Montgomery, AL 36103
Alabama Mountain Lakes Tourist Association	www.northalabama.org	256-350-3500 800-648-5381	25062 North St. P.O. Box 1075, Mooresville, AL 35649
Alabama Travel Council	www.alabamatravel.org	334-271-0050	516 Oliver Road P.O. Box 210729, Montgomery, AL 36121
Bed and Breadfast Association of Alabama	www.bedandbreakfastalabama.com	N/A	P.O. Box 707, Montgomery, AL 36101
Colbert County Tourism and Convention Bureau	www.colbertcountytourism.org	256-383-0783 800-344-0783	P.O. Box 740425 Tuscumbia, AL 35674
Decatur-Morgan County Convention and Visitors Bureau	www.decaturcvb.org	256-350-2028 800-232-5449	719 Sixth Ave. S.E. P.O. Box 2349, Decatur, AL 35602
DeKalb County Tourist Association	www.tourdekalb.com	256-845-3957 888-805-4740	1503 Glenn Blvd. S.W. P.O. Box 681165, Fort Payne, AL 35968
Florence/Lauderdale Tourism	www.flo-tour.org	256-740-4141 888-356-8687	One Hightower Place Florence, AL 35630
Gadsden-Etowah Tourism Board	www.gadsden-etowahtourismboard.com	256-549-0351 888-565-0411	P.O. Box 8269 Gasden, AL 35902

Huntsville-Madison County Convention and Visitors Bureau	www.huntsville.org	256-551-2230	500 Church St. Suite One, Huntsville, AL 35801
Jackson County Tourism	www.jacksoncountychamber.com	256-259-5500 800-259-5508	407 E. Willow St. Scottsboro, AL 35768
Marshall County Convention and Visitors Bureau	www.marshallcountycvb.com	256-582-7015 800-582-6282	200 Gunter Ave. P.O. Box 711, Guntersville, AL 35976

Selected Alabama Attractions and Locations

Alabama Music Hall of Fame	www.alamhof.org	256-381-4417 800-239-2643	P.O. Box 740405 Tuscumbia, AL 35674
Ave Maria Grotto	www.avemariagrotto.com	256-734-4110 800-722-0999	1600 St. Bernard Drive S.E. Cullman, AL 35055
Bankhead National Forest	www.fs.fed.us/r8/alabama	205-489-5111	1070 Highway 33 N. P.O. Box 278, Double Springs, AL 35553
Burritt on the Mountain	www.burrittmuseum.com	256-536-2882	3101 Burritt Drive Huntsville, AL 35801
Cathedral Caverns	www.alapark.com	256-728-8193 800-252-7275	637 Cave Road Woodville, AL 35776
Cook's Science Museum	www.cookspest.com/museum.html	256-350-9347	412 13th St. S.E. Decatur, AL 35601
Coon Dog Cemetery	www.colbertcountytourism.org	256-383-0783 800-344-0783	P.O. Box 740425 Tuscumbia, AL 35674
Constitution Village	www.earlyworks.com	256-564-8100	109 Gates Ave. Huntsville, AL 35801
Covered Bridges of Blount County	www.coveredbridge.org	205-274-2153	227 Second Ave. E. P.O. Box 1487, Oneonta, AL 35121
DeSoto State Park	www.desotostatepark.com	256-845-0051	13883 County Road 89 Fort Payne, AL 35967
Dismals	www.dismalscanyon.com	205-993-4559	901 Highway 8 Phil Campbell, AL 35581
EarlyWorks Children's Museum	www.earlyworks.com	256-564-8100	404 Madison St. Huntsville, AL 35801
Fort Payne Depot Museum	www.warehouse-media.com/depot	256-845-5714	105 Fifth St. P.O. Box 681420, Fort Payne, AL 35968
Gorham's Bluff	www.gorhamsbluff.com	256-451-8439 256-451-2787	101 Gorham Drive, Gorham's Bluff Pisgah, AL 35765-6891
Harrison Brothers Hardware	www.harrisonbrothershardware.com	256-536-3631 800-533-3631	124 South Side Square Huntsville, AL 35801
Hindu Cultural Center of North Alabama	www.hccna.org	256-771-7772	14854 Smith Drive Harvest, AL 35752
Huntsville Botanical Garden	www.hsvbg.org	256-830-4447	4747 Bob Wallace Ave. Huntsville, AL 35805
Huntsville Museum of Art	www.hsvmuseum.org	256-535-4350 800-786-9095	300 Church St. S. Hunstville, AL 35801
Huntsville Railroad Depot and Museum	www.earlyworks.com	256-564-8100	320 Church St. Huntsville, AL 35801
Ivy Green The Birthplace of Helen Keller	www.helenkellerbirthplace.org	256-383-4066 888-329-2124	300 W. North Commons Tuscumbia, AL 35674
Jerry Brown Pottery	www.jerrybrownpottery.com	205-921-9483 800-341-4919	1414 County Highway 81 Hamilton, AL 35570

Jesse Owens Memorial Park	www.jesseowensmuseum.org	256-974-3636	7019 County Road 203 Danville, AL 35619
Little River National Preserve	www.nps.gov/liri	256-845-9605	2141 Gault Ave. N. Fort Payne, AL 35967
Natural Bridge of Alabama	www.northalabama.org	205-486-5330	Highway 278 W. Natural Bridge, AL 35577
Noccalula Falls Park	www.noccalulafalls.org	256-543-7412	1500 Noccalula Falls Park P.O. Box 267, Gadsden, AL 35999
North Alabama Birding Trail	www.northalabamabirdingtrail.com	256-350-3500 800-648-5381	25062 North St., P.O. Box 1075 Mooresville, AL 35649
Oakville Indian Mounds Education Center	home.hiwaay.net/~lcc/oimpm.htm	256-905-2494	1219 County Road 187 Danville, AL 35619
Old State Bank Building	www.decaturcvb.org	256-350-5060	P.O. Box 582 Decatur, AL 35602
Pope's Museum and Tavern	www.flo-tour.org	256-760-6439	203 Hermitage Drive Florence, AL 35630
Robert Trent Jones Golf Trail	www.rtjgolf.com	800-949-4444	SunBelt Golf Corp, 167 SunBelt Pkwy Birmingham, AL 35211
Rosenbaum House	www.wrightinalabama.com	256-740-8899	601 Riverview Drive Florence, AL 35630
Russell Cave National Monument	www.nps.gov/ruca	256-495-2672	3729 County Road 98 Bridgeport, AL 35740
Sand Mountain Stockyard	www.sandmountainstockyard.com	256-561-3434	19509 Alabama Highway 68 Crossville, AL 35962-4162
Shrine of the Most Blessed Sacrament	www.olamshrine.com	256-352-6267	3222 County Road 548 Hanceville, AL 35077
Skydive Alabama	www.skydivecullman.com	877-826-3367 866-345-5867	231 County Road 1360 Vinemont, AL 35179
Stevenson Railroad Depot	stevensondepotmuseum.com	256-437-3012	207 W. Main St. P.O. Box 894, Stevenson, AL 35772
Unclaimed Baggage Center	www.unclaimedbaggage.com	256-259-1525	509 W. Willow St. Scottsboro, AL 35768
U.S. Space and Rocket Center	www.spacecamp.com	256-837-3400 800-637-7223	1 Tranquility Base Huntsville, AL 35805
Walls of Jericho	www.jacksoncountychamber.com	256-259-5500	407 E. Willow St. Scottsboro, AL 35768
Weeden House Museum	www.huntsville.org	256-536-7718	300 Gates Ave. Huntsville, AL 35801
Wheeler National Wildlife Refuge	www.fws.gov/wheeler	256-353-7243	2700 Refuge Headquarters Road Decatur, AL 35603

Selected Alabama Festivals and Events

Alabama Gourd Festival	www.alabamagourdsociety.org	256-747-1447 800-313-5114	504 Fifth St. S.W. Cullman, AL 35055
Alabama Jubilee Hot Air Balloon Classic and Races	www.alabamajubilee.net	256-350-2028 800-524-6181	P.O. Box 2601 Decatur, AL 35602
Alabama Renaissance Faire	www.flo-tour.org	256-768-3031 888-356-8687	One Hightower Place Florence, AL 35630
Art on the Lake	www.lakeguntersville.org	256-582-4378	200 Gunter Ave., P.O. Box 577 Guntersville, AL 35976

Big Spring Jam	www.bigspringjam.org	256-551-2359	700 Monroe St. Huntsville, AL 35801
Bloomin' Festival	www.bloominfestival.com	256-739-6682 800-722-0999	1600 Saint Bernard Drive S.E. Cullman, AL 35055
Chicken and Egg Festival	www.lawrencealabama.com	256-974-2464	12001 Alabama Highway 157 P.O. Box 325, Moulton, AL 35650
Christmas in the Park	www.arabcity.org	256-586-3138 888-403-2722	1157 N. Main St. Arab, AL 35016
Eagle Awareness Program	www.alapark.com	256-571-5444	7966 Alabama Highway 227 Guntersville, AL 35976
Galaxy of Lights	www.hsvbg.org	256-830-4447	4747 Bob Wallace Ave. Huntsville, AL 35805
Great Moonbuggy Race	moonbuggy.msfc.nasa.gov	256-544-0632	N/A
Harvest Festival	www.boazchamberofcommerce.com	256-593-8154	100 E. Bartlett Ave. Boaz, AL 35957
Helen Keller Festival	www.helenkellerfestival.com	256-383-0783 800-344-0783	One Hightower Place Florence, AL 35630
Indian Burial Mounds Festival	www.lawrencealabama.com	256-905-2494	12001 Alabama Highway 157 P.O. Box 325, Moulton, AL 35650
Living Christmas Tree	www.fbchsv.org/lct	256-428-9422	600 Governor's Drive Huntsville, AL 35801
Maple Hill Cemetery Stroll	www.huntsvillepilgrimage.org	256-551-2283 800-772-2348	202 Maple Hill Drive Huntsville, AL 35801
Moontown Air Show	www.moontownairport.com	256-852-9781	200 Airport Dr. Brownsboro, Al 35741
North Alabama Scottish Festival and Highland Games	www.tvss.org	256-519-2787	P.O. Box 1983 Huntsville, AL 35807
Old Time Fiddlers' Convention	www.athens.edu/fiddlers	256-233-8100	101 S. Beaty St. P.O. Box 150, Athens, AL 35612
Panoply	www.panoply.org	256-519-2787	700 Monroe St. Huntsville, AL 35801
Parent/Child Weekend at U.S. Space Camp	www.spacecamp.com	256-837-3400 800-637-7223	1 Tranquility Base Huntsville, AL 35805
Poke Salat Festival	www.marshallcountycvb.com	256-586-9913	200 Gunter Ave., P.O. Box 711 Guntersville, AL 35976
Racking Horse World Celebration	www.rackinghorse.com www.decaturcvb.org	256-353-7225	67 Horse Center Road Decatur, AL 35603
Riverfest Barbeque Cookoff	www.decaturcvb.org	800-524-6181	719 Sixth Ave. S.E., P.O. Box 2349 Decatur, AL 35602
Santa's Village	www.earlyworks.com	256-564-8100 800-678-1819	109 Gates Ave. Huntsville, AL 35801
Seafood Festival	www.stwilliamchurch.com/festival	256-582-4245	929 Gunter Ave. Guntersville, AL 35976
Siege at Bridgeport Civil War Reenactment	www.siegeatbridgeport.com	256-495-3614 800-259-5508	P.O. Box 280 Bridgeport, AL 35740
Spirit of America	www.decaturcvb.org	256-350-2028 800-524-6181	719 Sixth Ave. S.E., P.O. Box 2349 Decatur, AL 35602
Tanner's Tractor Pull	www.tourathens.com	256-232-2600	101 S. Beaty St. P.O. Box 150, Athens, AL 35612

Tim's Cajun Kitchen Crawfish Festival	www.timscajunkitchen.com	256-533-7589	114 Jordan Lane Huntsville, AL 35805
Trail of Tears Commemorative Motorcycle Ride	www.al-tn-trailoftears.org	256-740-4141 888-356-8687	P.O. Box 10081 Huntsville, AL 35801
W.C. Handy Music Festival	www.wchandymusicfestival.org	256-766-7642 800-472-5837	217 E. Tuscaloosa St. Florence, AL 35630
World's Longest Yard Sale	www.127sale.com	256-549-0351 888-565-0411	P.O. Box 8269 Gasden, AL 35902

Abandoning Family Members at Rest Stops Strictly Prohibited

About the Authors

Yoda

Technical Advisor

52 Weekends in the Tennessee Valley is a collaborative effort between father and son. In addition to residing in and exploring the Tennessee Valley, the Frew family has lived in Europe, the Near East, the Middle East and the Far East.

Charles (Chuck) is a graduate of the University of Alabama (School of Law, 1968). He was an Army JAG Officer and is a retired government attorney. Chuck currently does part-time consulting work.

Daniel is a graduate of Auburn University (1999) where he majored in visual communications. Daniel works as a graphic designer and art director.

It has been reliably reported that neither family member died as a result of this domestic bonding experience.

"Twenty years from now you will be more disappointed by the things you didn't do than by the ones you did do."

Mark Twain